the SNOWFLAKE Book of Baking

the SNOWFLAKE Book of Baking

STRUIK

Struik Publishers (Pty) Ltd
(a member of The Struik Publishing Group (Pty) Ltd)
Cornelis Struik House
80 McKenzie Street
Cape Town 8001

Reg. No.: 54/00965/07

First published in 1994
Second impression February 1995
Third impression June 1995
Fourth impression November 1995
Fifth impression April 1996
Sixth impression September 1996

Copy compiled by: Heilie Voges
Recipes tested at different altitudes by: Luiza Rigutto and Marlene van Staden
Editor: Elizabeth Frost
Designer: Rob House
Indexer: Sandie Vahl
Cover design: Rob House
Illustrator: Royston Lamond

Photographer: Willie van Heerden
Styling: Heilie Voges and Myrna Klerck
Food preparation: Heilie Voges, Myrna Klerck and Frieda Minnaar
Typing of original copy: Shantellé Parker

Typesetting by Struik DTP, Cape Town
Reproduction by Unifoto (Pty) Ltd, Cape Town
Printing and binding by Times Offset (M) Sdn Bhd

ISBN 1 86825 641 3

Acknowledgements
Premier Milling would like to extend grateful thanks to the team at Struik Publishers, and to the following companies for the loan of crockery and props for the photography:

Stuttafords, Eastgate and Westgate
The Crockery Warehouse, Auckland Park
Sanitary City, Midrand
Taung Marble, Bramley

Contents

Introduction

Introduction

ALL THE RECIPES INCLUDED IN THIS BOOK HAVE BEEN TESTED USING VARIOUS SNOWFLAKE FLOURS TO ENSURE BEST RESULTS AND FRESHNESS. THE SNOWFLAKE BOOK OF BAKING IS INTENDED FOR EVERYDAY USE AND THEREFORE INCLUDES SIMPLE AND ECONOMICAL RECIPES WITHIN THE REACH OF EVERYONE. EXPERIENCED AND INEXPERIENCED COOKS ALIKE WILL BE ABLE TO ACHIEVE SUCCESS.

WHEAT

Wheat is one of the world's most important sources of food and is widely cultivated in all types of climates. It is relied upon as a staple food by a large part of the world's population.

The nutrients found in wheat are carbohydrates (starch), proteins, lipids, minerals and vitamins. These are stored in the wheat kernel, which is comprised of the following:

- Bran, the outer shell, which needs to be removed to produce pure flour. It contains a high proportion of roughage, is rich in minerals and plays a role in aiding digestion and preventing constipation.

- Endosperm is the usable inner part of the kernel. It is separated from the bran and crushed into a powder to form flour. An important source of starch, it provides warmth and energy.

- Germ, which is the beginning of the new wheat plant, is normally removed as its fat content has adverse effects on the flour-making process. The fat limits the keeping quality of flour – a good reason for storing wheat germ in the refrigerator.

The milling process

The raw wheat is conveyed to separators, which remove the straws, sticks and unwanted seeds so that only pure wheat passes on to be washed. Once washed, the wheat is whisked dry in a type of spin-drier and transported to storage bins.

Once blended, the wheat is ready to be milled and is conveyed to roller mills. After the wheat has passed through the first roller mill – this is known as the first break – it emerges as crushed wheat. Once the wheat has moved through various breaking and reducing systems, it is sifted. This separates particles of different sizes, which are then passed on to the purifiers. These grade the mixture according to particle size and purity. The various products are then weighed and packed. The wheat remains untouched by human hands throughout the entire milling process.

TYPES OF SNOWFLAKE FLOUR

To obtain the best use out of this book it is important to get to know the various flours that are available from Snowflake by trying and testing them. Whichever kind of flour you use for baking, remember that the moisture content of freshly packaged flour will be correct and results will probably be more reliable.

TYPES OF FLOUR AND THEIR SNOWFLAKE EQUIVALENTS

All-purpose flour	**Snowflake cake flour**
Strong plain flour	**Snowflake cake flour**
Ordinary plain flour	**Snowflake white bread flour**
Strong white flour	**Snowflake cake flour**
Flour	**Snowflake cake flour**
Wholemeal flour	**Snowflake Nutty Wheat meal**

Cake flour

This is made from the purest, whitest part of the wheat, which is ground down very finely and then sifted through fine nylon sieves. Snowflake cake flour is of a very high standard, has a high protein content, is unbleached and contains no additives.

The protein found in flour is called gluten. It is the gluten in the flour that holds the mixture together.

Cake flour is suitable for many purposes, such as making confectionery, special bread, pastries and biscuits. It can be stored for 6–8 months under ideal conditions, and up to 1 year in a refrigerator or deep-freeze.

Self-raising flour

This is cake flour to which a raising agent has been added in order to give lightness to the baked product. It is used for quick-mix and baked products such as scones, waffles, cakes and biscuits. Once the packet has been opened, it should be stored in an airtight container so that the raising agent remains fresh.

If self-raising flour is required and none is available, use 250 ml plain cake flour and 5 ml baking powder, sifted together, to make 250 ml self-raising flour.

For wholemeal self-raising flour, add 5 ml baking powder to every 250 ml plain wholemeal flour. Sift together several times before using.

Store self-raising flour for 6–8 months under ideal conditions, and for up to 1 year in a refrigerator or deep-freeze.

White bread flour

This is a pure wheaten product that is not as white as cake flour. It is used by commercial bakeries to produce white bread.

It can be used for making loaf-type cakes, fruit cakes, pizza doughs, rusks and as a thickening agent in gravies and stews.

White bread flour can be stored for 6–8 months under ideal conditions, and for 1 year in a refrigerator or deep-freeze.

Clockwise from top left: Digestive bran, Self-raising Flour, Brown Bread Meal, Nutty Wheat, White Bread Flour, Cake Flour. Centre: Semolina.

Brown bread meal

Brown bread meal is made from white bread flour to which approximately 12 per cent fine wheaten bran (a valuable source of fibre) has been added. Brown bread meal is used by commercial bakeries to bake brown bread and domestically for making pastry, bread and scones.

Store brown bread meal for up to 4 months under ideal conditions, and for up to 1 year in a refrigerator or deep-freeze.

Wholewheat meal (Nutty Wheat)

Wholewheat meal, also known as 'Nutty Wheat', is made from white bread flour to which about 20 per cent coarse wheaten bran has been added. Used in scones, breads, pastries and rusks, wholewheat meal is the most healthy of all the flours as it has a high fibre content, which is an essential part of one's diet.

Due to the presence of wheat germ, wholewheat meal has an oil content and therefore cannot be stored as long as the white flours. In hot, humid conditions it is advisable to store the flour in a refrigerator.

When using wholewheat meal on its own in baking, bear in mind that the baked product will be slightly heavier than usual. If you require a lighter texture, substitute half the quantity of wholewheat meal with cake or white bread flour.

Store Nutty Wheat for up to 3 months under ideal conditions, and for up to 1 year in a refrigerator or deep-freeze.

Semolina

This is a pure wheaten product in granular form that is used commercially for making spaghetti and noodles, and is also ideal for porridges and puddings. Store for 6–8 months under ideal conditions, and for up to 1 year in a refrigerator or deep-freeze.

Digestive bran

The outer layer of the wheat kernel is removed to produce bran, which is an unrefined by-product of flour. It is rich in cellulose, a fibre product, and in vitamins and minerals. It can be added to breads, scones and muesli and sprinkled over porridge and cereal. Store for 3 months under ideal conditions, and up to 1 year in a refrigerator or deep-freeze.

STORING FLOUR

- Because flour readily absorbs foreign flavours and odours, it is essential to store it in a clean, airtight container in a cool, dry place, away from products with a strong flavour or odour. Buy enough flour for the short term only, especially if you live in a hot area, where weevils and worm infestation are common. Do not add fresh flour to old flour.

- Place a bayleaf in the flour to prevent weevils.

- Every packet of Snowflake flour is stamped with a 'sell by' date, which guarantees the freshest possible product for the consumer, and should be used as a guide to the age of the flour. The flour may be used for 6–8 months after the date has expired.

- Store flour in an airtight container in a refrigerator or deep-freeze for up to 1 year. Return to room temperature an hour before using.

- The amount of liquid given in a recipe may have to be adjusted according to the age of the flour – the fresher the flour, the less liquid you will need; the older the flour, the more liquid you will need.

USEFUL HINTS

Correct measuring

Ingredients should be measured or weighed very accurately. To ensure success, use standard metric measuring equipment, such as a set of cups, as ordinary teacups or tablespoons will vary in size from consumer to consumer. Sets comprising a standard 250 ml cup, ½ cup, ⅓ cup and ¼ cup are available. (See Conversion Chart, opposite page.) Standard sets of spoons are available in 15 ml, 5 ml, 2 ml and 1 ml sizes. Measuring jugs are used for measuring liquid in millilitres.

How to use the recipes

First read the recipe carefully. Ingredients in recipes always appear in the order in which they are used. For best results in baking, use ingredients at room temperature, unless stated otherwise. Collect and measure all the ingredients, prepare baking tins and set the oven to the correct temperature before beginning.

INGREDIENTS

Flour

To measure flour correctly, spoon the unsifted flour gently into the measuring cup, without pressing down. Shake the cup slightly and level off with a knife or spatula, then sift the flour once before starting to mix, as this will ensure light results.

Cake flour, self-raising flour, white bread flour and semolina should be sifted. Brown bread meal and wholewheat meal are also sifted, and the bran left behind in the sieve is tipped back into the flour. Digestive bran cannot be sifted and is therefore just added to the ingredients.

Baking powder

In ideal conditions, store a tin of commercial baking powder for 1 year. To extend its shelf life, store baking powder in the refrigerator or deep-freeze.

Eggs

All the recipes in this book were tested using large eggs (51–61 g). Eggs determine the colour, flavour, lightness and binding of the cake mixture, as well as its nutritional value. To ensure freshness, buy small quantities of eggs at a time. Work with eggs that are at room temperature; this will enable you to beat them to a greater volume. When creaming, always add the eggs one at a time and beat well after each addition.

Shortening (margarine/butter)

Either margarine or butter can be used in baking, but where butter is specifically referred to in recipes such as those for pastries, it cannot be replaced by margarine. Butter gives the best flavour, especially to a sponge cake. When baking with margarine, use brick margarine and not the tub variety, as the latter contains more water and can easily be over-creamed. In some sponge cakes oil is used.

Chilled margarine or butter is required for pastries and rubbing in. When rubbing into flour, use your fingertips as these are the coolest part of your hands.

For accurate and easy use, measuring is done in grams. Take margarine or butter out of the refrigerator at least an hour prior to baking. It will then be fairly soft and facilitate easy creaming.

Sugar

White granulated sugar has been used, unless castor sugar or brown sugar is stated. Castor sugar is finer and therefore creams more easily. If no castor sugar is available, grind granulated sugar in a blender or food processor for a few seconds to give a finer texture. When creaming margarine and sugar together, add the sugar a little at a time and cream using either a wooden spoon or an electric mixer. Adding the sugar slowly and gradually will make it possible for the sugar to dissolve

SUBSTITUTES

230 g butter/margarine	**220 ml cooking oil**
15 ml cornflour	**30 ml cake flour**
15 ml/10 g instant dry yeast	**25 g fresh cube yeast**
250 ml sugar	**200 ml golden syrup or honey**
250 ml sour milk	**250 ml milk plus 20 ml lemon juice or vinegar**
250 ml sour cream	**250 ml cream plus 20 ml lemon juice or vinegar**

more easily. Once all the sugar has been added, beat the mixture until it is light and fluffy. Most of the sugar will dissolve in the creaming process. This will ensure a light texture in a cake or biscuit.

Liquid

Liquid is essential in baking. Apart from combining the ingredients, the liquid forms steam and aids the rising of cakes. Use water, milk, fruit juices and wines at room temperature, unless otherwise stated in the recipe. Measure accurately by placing the measuring jug on a flat surface and checking the meniscus level. This will ensure the right consistency in a mixture. Do not add all the liquid at once, but pour slowly into the dry ingredients.

PREHEATING THE OVEN

Before preheating your oven, adjust the shelves to the required level. The temperatures and baking times given in these recipes are only a guideline. Get to know your oven and adjust the temperatures and times accordingly. Switch the oven on at least 10 minutes before baking and set it about 5–10 degrees higher than the temperature required, as when you open the oven door, hot air will escape and the temperature will drop. After placing the cake in the oven, turn the temperature to the correct setting.

Level of shelves in oven for baking

- The oven is slightly warmer at the top than it is lower down. Pastries are baked, and grilling and toasting are done, on the top and second shelves.
- Bake small cakes or biscuits one shelf above the middle shelf.
- The heat is very even in the middle of the oven and general baking of cakes, breads and biscuits, for example, is done here.
- Large cakes and rich fruit cakes should be baked one shelf below the middle shelf.
- The bottom of the oven is slightly cooler and should be used for slow cooking, for example meringues as well as for drying rusks.

QUICK CONVERSIONS

	¼ cup	½ cup	¾ cup	1 cup
METRIC	65 ML	125 ML	190 ML	250 ML
Cake flour	35 g	70 g	105 g	140 g
Self-raising flour	35 g	70 g	105 g	140 g
White bread flour	35 g	70 g	105 g	140 g
Brown bread meal	35 g	70 g	105 g	140 g
Nutty Wheat	30 g	75 g	115 g	150 g
Semolina	40 g	80 g	120 g	160 g
Digestive bran	8 g	15 g	22 g	30 g
Sugar – white and brown	50 g	100 g	150 g	200 g
Castor sugar	55 g	105 g	160 g	210 g
Icing sugar	35 g	65 g	100 g	130 g
Butter/margarine	60 g	115 g	175 g	230 g
Raisins and sultanas	40 g	75 g	115 g	150 g
Coconut	20 g	40 g	60 g	80 g

GRAM WEIGHT PER 250 ML

All Bran Flakes/Cornflakes	50
Biscuit crumbs	120
Butter	230
Cake crumbs, fresh	125
CHEESE:	
Cheddar, grated	100
Cottage and cream cheese	250
Mozzarella, grated	125
Coconut, desiccated	80
Choc bits	200
Custard powder	120
Digestive bran	30
DRIED FRUIT:	
Apricots	150
Cherries, cut	150
Cherries, whole	160
Dates	150
Fruit cake mix	150
Mixed peel	150
Prunes, stoned	150
Raisins, sultanas, currants	150
FLOUR:	
Brown bread meal	140
Cake flour	140
Cornflour	120
Crushed wheat	200
Nutty Wheat (wholewheat meal)	150
Self-raising flour	140
Semolina	160
Wheatgerm	80
White bread flour	140
Ham, chopped	125
Jam, apricot	330
Margarine	230
NUTS:	
Almonds, shelled, flaked	150
Peanuts, shelled	150
Pecans, walnuts	100
Sprinkle nuts	150
Oats	80
SEED:	
Poppy	150
Sesame	150
Sunflower	150
SUGAR:	
Castor sugar	210
Icing sugar	130
White sugar	200
Yellow and brown sugar	200
VEGETABLES:	
Carrots, grated	125
Mushrooms	70
Potatoes, grated raw	125
Pumpkin, cooked and mashed	225
Spinach	200

ALTITUDE BAKING

For the purposes of this book, all recipes were tested on the highveld as well as at sea level. The following chart is therefore not necessary for recipes in this book, but can be used to make adjustments in other recipes you may have. High altitude recipes can be used in reverse.

ALTITUDE	900 m (3000 ft)	1500 m (5000 ft)	2100 m (7000 ft)	3000 m (10000 ft)
Temperature	Increase by 5 °C/25 °F	Increase by 10 °C/50 °F	Increase by 10 °C/50 °F	Increase by 10 °C/50 °F
Baking powder per 1 tsp	Reduce by 0–0,5 ml	Reduce by 1 ml	Reduce by 1 ml	Reduce by 1 ml
Sugar per cup	Reduce by 0–15 ml	Reduce by 15–30 ml	Reduce by 30–45 ml	Reduce by 30–45 ml
Liquid per cup	Increase by 0–30 ml	Increase by 30–45 ml	Increase by 45–60 ml	Increase by 45–60 ml
Flour per cup			Increase by 15 ml	Increase by 15 ml

CAKE TIN SIZES

1 Cake tin	20 cm
2 Loaf tin	23 cm
3 Loose-bottomed tart tin	24 cm
4 Pizza plate	25 cm
5 Swiss roll tin	23 cm x 32 cm
6 Loose-bottomed cake tin	20 cm
7 Ring tin	22 cm
8 Fancy flan tin	24 cm
9 Rectangular tin	20 cm x 24 cm
10 Deep square cake tin	20 cm

CONVERSIONS

VOLUME

METRIC	IMPERIAL
1 ml	pinch
2 ml	¼ teaspoon
3 ml	½ teaspoon
5 ml	1 teaspoon
15 ml	1 tablespoon
80 ml	⅓ cup
170 ml	⅔ cup
250 ml	1 cup
315 ml	1 ¼ cups
375 ml	1 ½ cups
440 ml	1 ¾ cups
500 ml	2 cups
750 ml	3 cups

WEIGHTS

METRIC	IMPERIAL
15 g	½ oz
30 g	1 oz
60 g	2 oz
90 g	3 oz
125 g	4 oz
150 g	5 oz
180 g	6 oz
210 g	7 oz
250 g	8 oz (½ lb)
500 g	1 lb
1 kg	2 lb

LIQUID CAPACITY

METRIC	IMPERIAL
30 ml	2 tablespoons
60 ml	4 tablespoons
150 ml	¼ pint
300 ml	½ pint
450 ml	¾ pint
600 ml	1 pint
900 ml	1,5 pints
1,25 litres	2 pints
1,8 litres	3 pints
2,5 litres	4 pints

Oven temperatures

	Celsius (C)	Fahrenheit (F)	Gas mark
Very low:	100 °C	200 °F	¼
	110 °C	225 °F	¼
	120 °C	250 °F	½
Low:	140 °C	275 °F	1
	150 °C	300 °F	2
Moderate:	160 °C	325 °F	3
	180 °C	350 °F	4
	190 °C	375 °F	5
	200 °C	400 °F	6
High:	220 °C	425 °F	7
	230 °C	450 °F	8
Very high:	240 °C	475 °F	9

Using a microwave

Get to know your microwave, as wattage differs from oven to oven, affecting baking and cooking.

Higher wattage microwave ovens (600 – 850 watts) are faster than the lower wattage ovens (400 – 500 watts). Ovens with a 650 wattage are more common, so most recipes are developed for these ovens. If your microwave oven is 600 watts, add 15 seconds to cooking time. For a 700 watt oven, subtract 5–10 seconds per minute.

Wattage and power

High	100% power
Medium-High	70% power
Medium	50% power
Medium-Low	30% power
Low	10% power

Testing equipment for microwaving

To establish whether cookware is suitable for microwave use, pour 250 ml cold water into a glass bowl or jug. Place this in the microwave, together with the dish to be tested. Microwave on High/100% power for 1 minute. The water in the jug should be warm, and the dish cool. If the dish is warm, it is not suitable for use in the microwave.

Important guidelines for microwaving

- Owing to the fact that ovens, cake mixtures and containers will differ, an exact time for baking cannot be given. A useful guideline to calculating the time needed for baking is to divide the time given for a conventional oven by four and then subtract a third.
- Lightly grease or spray the container. Place a piece of paper towel cut to size on the base. Do not flour the container.
- Cakes cook better on Medium-High/70% power or Medium/50% power.
- Take care not to overbake cakes. Remove from oven when just baked and test with a skewer.
- Muffins can be baked in paper cup cases on Medium-High/70% power for 3–4 minutes (six muffins). Place the paper case in a microwave muffin container or tea cup.
- Bake scones on a preheated browning dish on High/100% for 30 seconds. Turn scones over and repeat.
- Fill pans only two-thirds full.
- Cupcakes are best baked on Medium/50% power. Do not fill more than half full.
- Cakes tend to rise higher than usual, so only fill containers half-way. Plastic containers give better results.

Handy tips

- Scald milk for use in custards and sauces by heating 600 ml milk on High/100% power for 2–3 minutes.
- Caramelize sugar by placing sugar and water in a heat-resistant bowl. Microwave on High/100% power for 5–7 minutes, until golden.
- Heat golden syrup/honey in a heat resistant bowl on High/100% power for 1–2 minutes for every 300 g.
- Soften brown sugar by placing in microwave with a wedge of apple. Heat, covered on High/100% power for 30–40 seconds.
- Liquefy crystallized honey by heating on High/100% power for 30 seconds. Stir until smooth, then microwave for a few more seconds.
- Toast desiccated coconut by microwaving 500 ml on High/100% power for 5–6 minutes. Stir frequently.
- To melt chocolate: Break into pieces and place in a heat-resistant bowl. Microwave on High/100 % power for about 1 minute per 100 g. Stir until smooth. Microwave for a few more seconds if still lumpy, taking care not to overheat, or the chocolate will burn.
- Soften 125 g butter on Medium-Low/30% power for 40 seconds.
- To reheat cooked pastries: Heat small pies on High/100% power for 10–30 seconds and larger pies for 2–3 minutes.
- To enable yeast dough to rise quickly (to prove): Place the dough in a bowl and cover with plastic wrap. Pour 1 litre of warm water into a large bowl. Place the bowl containing the water alongside. Microwave on Low/10% power for 10 minutes. Allow to rest for 15 minutes. Repeat until dough has doubled in size.
- To defrost a loaf of bread: Wrap in damp paper towel and defrost on Medium-Low/30% power for 4 minutes, depending on the size of the loaf.
- To defrost a slice of bread: Wrap in damp paper towel and heat on High/100% power for 10–15 seconds.

1

Savouries and Snacks

Many of these quick-and-easy savouries and snacks can also be served as light meals, and most can be conveniently prepared in advance and heated when required. Versatile pizzas, savoury tarts and quiches can be made in different sizes with a variety of toppings and, served individually, are ideal as starters. As an ordinary bread or scone dough is used, pizzas couldn't be easier to make – and the results are excellent!

MUSHROOM AND BACON QUICHE

PASTRY
250 ml Snowflake cake flour (140 g)
250 ml grated Cheddar cheese (100 g)
125 g butter

FILLING
250 g rindless streaky bacon, chopped
15 ml butter
200 g mushrooms, sliced
3 eggs
250 ml milk or fresh cream
125 ml sour cream
15 ml lemon juice
50 ml grated Parmesan cheese
3 ml mustard powder
3 ml salt
freshly ground black pepper to taste
6 ml chopped fresh herbs OR
2 ml mixed dried herbs

❶ For pastry: Mix all ingredients to a soft pastry in a food processor.

❷ Press into base and sides of 24 cm quiche dish.

❸ For filling: Fry bacon until crisp. Remove and keep aside. Add butter to rendered fat. Add mushrooms and sauté; spoon bacon and mushrooms onto base. Beat eggs, milk, sour cream and lemon juice. Add Parmesan cheese and seasoning; pour onto base.

❹ Bake in a preheated oven at 160 °C (325 °F) for 45 minutes.

Serves 4–6

Tip

The difference between quiches and savoury tarts is that quiches have a savoury egg custard mixture as a base, whereas savoury tarts can have a starch, such as cornflour or flour, with or without an egg, to bind the mixture.

SALMON AND LEEK QUICHE

PASTRY
250 ml Snowflake cake flour (140 g)
250 ml grated Cheddar cheese (100 g)
125 g butter

FILLING
15 ml butter
4 leeks, sliced
2 cloves garlic, crushed
213 g can pink salmon, flaked
3 eggs
250 ml milk or fresh cream
125 ml sour cream
15 ml lemon juice
3 ml salt
freshly ground black pepper to taste
6 ml chopped fresh herbs OR
2 ml mixed dried herbs

❶ For pastry: Mix all ingredients to a soft pastry in a food processor.

❷ Press into base and sides of 24 cm quiche dish.

❸ For filling: Heat butter and sauté leeks and garlic. Mix in salmon and spoon onto base. Beat eggs, milk, sour cream and lemon juice. Add seasoning and pour onto base.

❹ Bake in a preheated oven at 160 °C (325 °F) for 45 minutes.

Tip

Clean leeks by cutting through the leek down its length, almost through the root, and again a second time, making a cross. Open out and wash thoroughly under cold running water. Cut into rings.

ASPARAGUS ONION TART

PASTRY
250 ml Snowflake cake flour (140 g)
5 ml salt
125 g margarine
225 g can cream-style sweetcorn

FILLING
5 medium onions, chopped
65 g margarine
375 ml grated Cheddar cheese (150 g)
2 ml salt
2 eggs, beaten
250 ml sour cream
410 g can asparagus (salad cuts), drained

❶ For pastry: Sift flour and salt. Rub in margarine until mixture resembles fine breadcrumbs. Add sweetcorn and mix well. Spread into base and sides of a greased 23 cm ovenproof pie dish.

❷ For filling: Sauté onion in margarine until transparent.

❸ Add remaining ingredients, mix well, and spoon onto prepared base.

❹ Bake in a preheated oven at 180 °C (350 °F) for 45–60 minutes, or until set and golden brown.

Serves 4–6

Tip

When peeling onions, prevent irritation of the eyes by peeling them under cold running water. Alternatively, place onions in cold water 30 minutes before peeling.

Clockwise from top right: Salmon and Leek Quiche, Asparagus Onion Tart and Mushroom and Bacon Quiche.

HAM AND PINEAPPLE PIZZA

BASE
500 ml Snowflake self-raising flour (280 g)
30 g margarine
about 200 ml milk

TOPPING
410 g can tomato and onion mix
15 ml chopped fresh origanum OR 5 ml dried
15 ml chopped fresh basil OR 5 ml dried
1 ml salt
2 cloves garlic, crushed, optional
freshly ground black pepper to taste
1 green pepper, seeded and thinly sliced
440 g can pineapple pieces, drained
500 ml chopped smoked ham (250 g)
500 ml grated mozzarella cheese (250 g) OR Cheddar cheese (200 g)

❶ For base: Sift flour and rub in margarine.

❷ Add milk and mix to form a soft dough.

❸ Divide dough in half and roll out to fit two greased 25 cm pizza plates or place on a large greased baking tray.

❹ For topping: Heat tomato and onion mix, seasoning and garlic in a saucepan. Simmer for a few minutes and spread onto base.

❺ Top with remaining ingredients and sprinkle with grated mozzarella or Cheddar cheese.

❻ Bake in a preheated oven at 200 °C (400 °F) for 20–25 minutes, or until golden brown.

Makes 2 large pizzas

VARIATION

Substitute ham with sliced pepperoni sausage.

TIP

If serving pizzas as snacks, cut into squares once cooked, or make small individual ones.

TOMATO AND MUSHROOM PIZZA

BASE
500 ml Snowflake white bread flour OR cake flour (280 g)
2 ml salt
3 ml sugar
8 ml instant dry yeast (5 g)
30 ml cooking oil
about 125 ml lukewarm water

TOPPING
410 g can tomato and onion mix
2 cloves garlic, crushed
1 green pepper, seeded and sliced
250 g fresh mushrooms, sliced
125 g salami slices
5 ml dried Italian seasoning OR dried origanum
5 ml salt
freshly ground black pepper to taste
250 ml grated mozzarella cheese (125 g) OR Cheddar cheese (100 g)

❶ For base: Sift flour and salt. Add sugar and dry yeast and mix.

❷ Add oil and enough lukewarm water to mix to a soft dough. Knead for 5–10 minutes until dough is smooth and elastic.

❸ Cover with oiled plastic wrap and leave in a warm place for 45 minutes to rise, until double in volume.

❹ Knock down and divide into two. Flatten and place each piece on a greased 25 cm pizza plate.

❺ For topping: Heat tomato and onion mix, add garlic and green pepper and simmer for a few minutes. Spread onto base. Top with remaining ingredients and sprinkle with grated cheese. Leave to rest for 20 minutes.

❻ Bake in a preheated oven at 200 °C (400 °F) for 20 minutes.

Makes 2 large pizzas

VARIATIONS

Substitute salami with chopped ham, bacon or tuna.

Add or substitute other ingredients of your choice, such as pineapple, shrimps, asparagus and olives.

TIP

Pizzas on a yeast dough base, baked or unbaked, can be frozen successfully for up to one month, provided topping ingredients are suitable for freezing. Bake frozen, cooked pizza in a preheated oven at 200 °C (400 °F) for 15 minutes and frozen uncooked pizza for 30 minutes.

MUSHROOMS IN BATTER

1 egg
250 ml milk
250 ml Snowflake self-raising flour (140 g)
10 ml mixed spice
5 ml salt
freshly ground black pepper to taste
1 clove garlic, crushed
250 g button mushrooms

❶ Whisk egg and milk together. Sift dry ingredients and add milk mixture and crushed garlic to dry ingredients.

❷ Beat until smooth and leave batter standing for 30 minutes. (Batter can be kept in fridge for 1–2 weeks.)

❸ Dip mushrooms in batter and deep-fry in hot oil until golden brown.

❹ Drain on paper towel.

Serves 4–6

VARIATION

Substitute mushrooms with onion rings, cauliflower florets or broccoli florets.

TIP

Keep garlic fresh by peeling and placing in a bottle. Cover with olive or sunflower oil. Replace lid and refrigerate until needed. The oil can also be used for flavouring salads and meat.

Clockwise from top right: Ham and Pineapple Pizza, Tomato and Mushroom Pizza and miniature Tomato and Mushroom Pizzas.

CHEESE TART

PASTRY
375 ml Snowflake cake flour (210 g)
2 ml salt
1 egg, beaten
100 g butter
about 50 ml water

FILLING
4 eggs, separated
250 ml fresh cream
250 ml chopped smoked ham (125 g)
300 ml grated Cheddar cheese (120 g)
2 ml paprika
2 ml mustard powder
15 ml chopped fresh herbs OR
5 ml mixed dried herbs
3 ml salt
freshly ground black pepper to taste

❶ For pastry: Sift flour and salt. Add beaten egg and mix well.

❷ Grate cold butter over mixture and knead lightly. Add water, if necessary, and mix to a soft dough.

❸ Cover pastry with oiled plastic wrap and leave to rest in the refrigerator for 30 minutes. Roll out thinly, line base and sides of a 23 cm pie dish with pastry and prick base. Cover and leave in the refrigerator while preparing the filling.

❹ For filling: Mix egg yolks, cream, ham, cheese and seasoning.

❺ Beat egg whites until soft peak stage and fold into egg yolk mixture.

❻ Pour onto base and bake in a preheated oven at 160 °C (325 °F) for 45 minutes. Cover with aluminium foil during baking if tart starts to brown.

Serves 4–6

TIP

Cheese can be grated and stored in an airtight container in the deep-freeze for up to 6 months.

CHEESE STRAWS

½ quantity Puff Pastry (page 32)
250 ml grated Cheddar cheese (100 g)
3 ml salt
2 ml cayenne pepper

❶ Roll out pastry in a rectangular shape, to a thickness of 3 mm.

❷ Sprinkle grated cheese, salt and pepper over two-thirds of pastry. Fold up like a business letter so that cheese is sandwiched between layers of pastry. Refrigerate for 30 minutes.

❸ Roll out to a thickness of 3 mm. Cut into strips of 1, 5 cm x 8 cm. Twist each one and place on a greased baking tray.

❹ Bake in a preheated oven at 200 °C (400 °F) for 10 minutes.

Makes about 70

CHEESE AIGRETTES

250 ml grated Cheddar cheese (100 g)
1 quantity Choux Pastry (page 34)
cooking oil for frying
cayenne pepper

❶ Add grated cheese to choux pastry.

❷ Fry teaspoonfuls in deep, hot oil for 3–5 minutes, or until golden brown.

❸ Drain on paper towel and sprinkle with cayenne pepper.

Makes 20

VARIATIONS

POTATO PUFFS

Add 1 medium mashed potato and 5 ml mixed dried herbs to ingredients.

MINCE AND SWEETCORN AIGRETTES

Omit cheese and add 150 g cooked topside mince and a 225 g can cream-style sweetcorn to pastry.

WASGOED-BONDELTJIES

500 g topside mince
15 ml cooking oil
1 onion, finely chopped
1 clove garlic, crushed
1 carrot, finely grated
1 potato, finely grated
5 ml ground allspice
7 ml salt
freshly ground black pepper to taste
200 ml meat stock
2 quantities Shortcrust Pastry (page 30) OR
2 quantities Soda-water Pastry (page 32)
whole cloves
cooking oil for frying

❶ Fry the meat in oil until its colour changes. Add the onion and garlic and sauté.

❷ Add carrot, potato, allspice, seasoning and meat stock and simmer for 15 minutes. Leave to cool.

❸ Roll out pastry to a thickness of 3 mm. Cut into 75 mm x 75 mm squares. Place a little meat mixture in centre. Fold the four corners towards the centre and secure with a clove.

❹ Deep-fry in oil until golden brown. Drain on paper towel and serve hot.

Makes 48

TIP

If the chopping board you are using smells of onion or garlic, mark one side of the board with a pen and chop them on that side only.

COCKTAIL SAUSAGE ROLLS

30 ml cooking oil
600 g topside mince
1 onion, finely chopped
3 slices white bread, soaked in water
5 ml salt
freshly ground black pepper to taste
1 ml ground cloves
2 ml ground coriander
1 beef stock cube
20 ml vinegar
1 quantity Soda-water Pastry (page 32) OR
1 quantity Hot-water Pastry (page 32)
beaten egg or milk to glaze

❶ Heat oil and fry mince until colour changes. Add onion and sauté slightly.

❷ Add soaked bread, seasoning, spices, stock cube and vinegar. Simmer for about 5 minutes. Leave to cool completely.

❸ Roll out pastry into a rectangular shape about 10 cm wide. Place meat in a line down the middle. Fold one side of pastry over meat. Brush edge with water and cover with other side of pastry. Brush with beaten egg or milk.

❹ Cut into sections of about 4 cm and bake in a preheated oven at 200 °C (400 °F) for 20 minutes.

Makes 48

TIP

Use 50 ml home-made stock instead of the stock cube, as stock cubes have a high salt content.

Clockwise from top: Cheese Straws, Cocktail Sausage Rolls, Wasgoedbondeltjies, Cheese Aigrettes and Mince and Sweetcorn Aigrettes.

VOL-AU-VENTS

1 quantity Puff Pastry (page 32)
beaten egg or milk to glaze

❶ Roll out pastry to a thickness of 3 mm. Use a 10 cm cutter to cut out 12–16 circles. Use a smaller cutter to cut out the centre of half of these circles to make lids.

❷ Brush edges of full circles with water. Place ones with centre cut out on top. Press down lightly.

❸ Brush with beaten egg or milk. Place on a greased baking tray and bake in a preheated oven at 200 °C (400 °F) for 20 minutes, until golden brown. Bake lids at the same time.

❹ Hollow out centre slightly and fill, placing lids on top.

Makes 6–8

VARIATION

Bouchées, a smaller version of vol-au-vents, are made in the same way, without the pastry lid.

> *TIP*
>
> *Before placing the vol-au-vent cases in the oven, prick each top layer four times with a skewer to ensure that the sides of the cases rise evenly.*

Mushroom and chicken filling

30 ml margarine
30 ml Snowflake cake flour
250 ml milk
100 g mushrooms, chopped
125 g cooked chicken, finely chopped
2 ml salt
freshly ground black pepper to taste

❶ Melt margarine in a saucepan. Add flour and stir over low heat for 1 minute. Remove from heat and add milk, stirring until smooth.

❷ Return to medium heat and stir constantly until boiling. Lower heat and cook for 5 minutes, stirring frequently until thickened.

❸ Add the mushrooms, chicken and seasoning. Fill vol-au-vents or bouchées and serve while still hot.

Tuna and cucumber filling

200 g can solid tuna, in vegetable oil, drained and flaked
½ English cucumber, diced
1 spring onion, chopped
about 75 ml mayonnaise
15 ml chopped fresh parsley OR
5 ml dried
pinch salt
freshly ground black pepper to taste

Mix all ingredients together and fill vol-au-vents.

BANANA BACON ROLLS

2 bananas
30 ml lemon juice
½ quantity Flaky Pastry (page 32)
125 g rindless streaky bacon rashers
beaten egg or milk to glaze

❶ Cut each banana in half horizontally and each half into five pieces. Dip pieces in lemon juice.

❷ Roll out pastry to a thickness of 3 mm. Cut into strips long enough to wrap around banana pieces.

❸ Wrap each piece of banana in a rasher of bacon and cover with pastry strip. Damp end with water to seal.

❹ Place on a greased baking tray and brush with beaten egg or milk.

❺ Bake in a preheated oven at 220 °C (425 °F) for 20 minutes. Serve hot.

Makes 20

> *TIP*
>
> *Pour boiling water over unpeeled banana to prevent discoloration.*

QUICK SAVOURY TART

250 g rindless streaky bacon, chopped
1 onion, chopped
250 g button mushrooms, sliced
15 ml butter
30 ml chopped fresh herbs OR
10 ml mixed dried herbs
freshly ground black pepper to taste
500 ml grated Cheddar cheese (200 g)
2 eggs
250 ml milk
50 ml Snowflake self-raising flour

❶ Fry bacon in a saucepan. Add onion, mushrooms and butter and sauté lightly.

❷ Add herbs and pepper to above ingredients and layer on bottom of a greased 18 cm x 28 cm ovenproof dish. Sprinkle with grated cheese.

❸ Beat eggs, milk and flour together and pour over ingredients in dish.

❹ Bake in a preheated oven at 180 °C (350 °F) for 30 minutes, or until set and golden brown.

Serves 4–6

> *TIP*
>
> *Fry streaky bacon by placing it in a cold frying pan, without fat. Cook over low heat, turning frequently, until done to your liking. For crisp bacon, pour off the fat as it collects.*

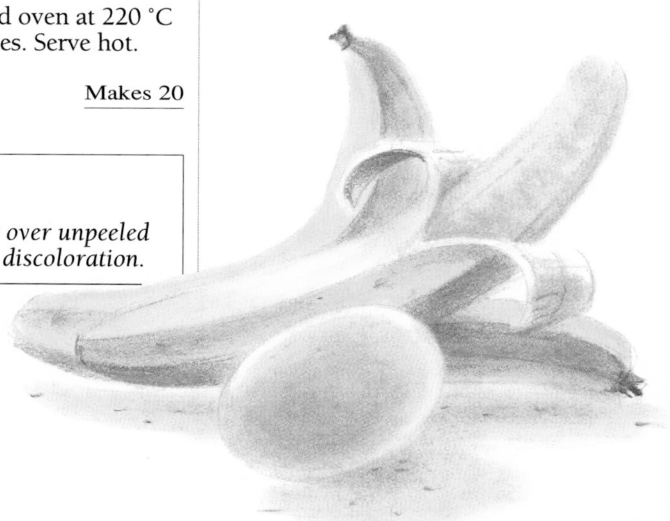

From top: Quick Savoury Tart, Banana Bacon Rolls, Bouchées and Vol-au-vents.

LIGHT MEALS

THE RECIPES IN THIS SECTION REQUIRE VERY LITTLE PREPARATION TIME AND PRODUCE TASTY, ECONOMICAL DISHES THAT ARE IDEAL FOR LIGHT SUPPERS OR LUNCHES – AND MANY WILL APPEAL TO THE WEIGHT-CONSCIOUS. INCLUDED ARE A VARIETY OF DELICIOUS HOME-MADE PIES – WHICH ARE ALWAYS NICER THAN COMMERCIALLY MADE – AS WELL AS FISH PIES, A SOUFFLÉ AND MINCE DISHES.

HADDOCK PIE

30 ml margarine
30 ml Snowflake cake flour
250 ml milk
250 g frozen haddock fillets, cooked and flaked
250 ml grated Cheddar cheese (100 g)
15 ml chopped gherkins
1 medium onion, finely chopped
15 ml chopped fresh parsley OR 5 ml dried
15 ml chopped fresh herbs OR 5 ml dried mixed herbs
5 ml mustard powder
2 ml salt
freshly ground black pepper to taste
3 eggs, beaten
1 quantity Cream Cheese Pastry (page 34)

❶ Melt margarine in a saucepan. Add flour and stir over low heat for 1 minute. Remove from heat and add milk, stirring until smooth.

❷ Return to medium heat and stir constantly until boiling. Lower heat and cook for 5 minutes, stirring frequently. Remove from heat.

❸ Add remaining ingredients, except pastry, to white sauce.

❹ Roll out pastry to a thickness of 3 mm and line a greased, round 23 cm pie dish.

❺ Spoon filling onto base and bake in a preheated oven at 180 °C (350 °F) for 30 minutes.

Serves 4–6

TIP

To cook haddock in the microwave: Place fish in a small dish and add a little water. Cover and microwave for 3–4 minutes on high or 100% power. Allow to stand, then drain and flake.

STEAK AND KIDNEY PIE

200 g calf or lamb's kidneys
500 g bolo or topside
15 ml butter
15 ml cooking oil
1 onion, chopped
375 ml meat stock
15 ml vinegar
5 ml salt
freshly ground black pepper to taste
15 ml chopped fresh herbs OR 5 ml mixed dried herbs
25 ml Snowflake cake flour
½ quantity Soda-water Pastry (page 32) OR ½ quantity Shortcrust Pastry (page 30)
beaten egg or milk to glaze

❶ Prepare kidneys: Make a small cut in the outer membrane and peel away from kidney. Slice kidney in half lengthways and cut out core with scissors or a sharp knife.

❷ Cut meat and kidneys into cubes and brown in heated butter and oil.

❸ Add onion and sauté. Add heated stock, vinegar and seasoning.

❹ Cover with lid and simmer for 30 minutes. Thicken with flour. Place filling in a medium pie dish or six small ones and leave to cool.

❺ Roll out pastry to a thickness of 3 mm and cover filling. Brush with beaten egg or milk. Bake in a preheated oven at 200 °C (400 °F) for 20 minutes.

Serves 4

CORNISH PASTIES

These pasties were originally developed in the 19th century in Cornwall, England, as a convenient lunch for tin miners to carry to work in their pockets. Each miner's initials were placed on a corner of the pasty so that, if called away during lunch time, he could return to his own pie.

250 g rump steak
1 medium carrot
1 medium potato
1 medium onion, chopped
15 ml chopped fresh parsley OR 5 ml dried
15 ml chopped fresh herbs OR 5 ml mixed dried herbs
5 ml salt
freshly ground black pepper to taste
30 ml butter
1 ½ quantities Shortcrust Pastry (page 30) OR 1 ½ quantities Hot-water Pastry (page 32)
beaten egg or milk to glaze

❶ Cut meat into cubes of 1,5 cm x 1,5 cm. Dice carrot and potato. Mix meat, vegetables and seasoning.

❷ Roll out pastry to a thickness of 3 mm. Use a saucer to cut out six circles, each about 20 cm in diameter.

❸ Divide meat mixture between pasties, placing it in the centre. Place 5 ml butter on each.

❹ Dampen edges of pastry with water, bring together over middle of filling, and seal to enclose filling.

❺ Place pasties on a greased baking tray and brush with beaten egg or milk. Bake in a preheated oven at 200 °C (400 °F) for 20 minutes. Reduce heat to 150 °C (300 °F) and bake a further 35 minutes.

Makes 6

TIP

If pastry browns too quickly, cover tops of pasties with foil.

Clockwise from top right: Haddock Pie, Cornish Pasties and Steak and Kidney Pie.

VEGETABLE MIX WITH DUMPLINGS

30 ml cooking oil
3 large potatoes, cut into cubes
2 medium onions, sliced
20 ml Snowflake cake flour
5 ml salt
freshly ground black pepper to taste
250 ml chicken stock
2 medium tomatoes, skinned and chopped
3 baby marrows, sliced
2 celery sticks, sliced
2 leeks, sliced
200 g button mushrooms, halved

HERB DUMPLINGS
250 ml Snowflake self-raising flour (140 g)
3 ml salt
30 g margarine
30 ml chopped fresh herbs OR
10 ml mixed dried herbs
about 125 ml milk or water to mix

❶ Heat oil and fry potatoes and onions until golden brown. Add flour, salt, pepper and chicken stock.

❷ Add remaining vegetables and simmer over low heat for 10 minutes.

❸ For dumplings: Sift flour and salt.

❹ Rub in margarine with fingertips until mixture resembles breadcrumbs. Add mixed herbs.

❺ Add enough milk to mix to a soft dough.

❻ Drop spoonfuls of dough onto boiling vegetables.

❼ Cover with lid and boil for another 15 minutes. Do not remove lid until dumplings are cooked.

Serves 4

VARIATIONS FOR DUMPLINGS

Add 5 ml curry powder to dry ingredients.

Add 3 ml crushed garlic to liquid for mixing.

Add 25 ml tomato purée or sauce to liquid for mixing.

MINCE ROLL

FILLING
30 ml cooking oil
400 g topside mince
1 onion, chopped
2 cloves garlic, crushed
salt and freshly ground black pepper to taste
30 ml chopped fresh parsley OR
10 ml dried
200 ml chutney

DOUGH
500 ml Snowflake self-raising flour (280 g)
2 ml salt
5 ml sugar
30 g margarine
125 ml grated Cheddar cheese (50 g)
1 egg
125 ml milk
beaten egg or milk to glaze

❶ For filling: Heat oil and fry mince until colour changes. Add onion and garlic and sauté a few minutes. Season with salt, pepper and parsley.

❷ Add chutney and leave to cool slightly.

❸ For dough: Sift flour, salt and sugar. Rub in margarine and add cheese.

❹ Beat egg and milk, add to dry ingredients, and mix to a soft dough.

❺ Roll out into a 20 cm x 30 cm rectangle. Spoon meat onto dough, roll up like a Swiss roll, and place on a greased baking tray. Make a few incisions in roll. Brush with beaten egg or milk.

❻ Bake in a preheated oven at 180 °C (350 °F) for 50 minutes.

Serves 4–6

TIP

Cut roll into 2,5 cm slices, freeze, and bake as required.

CHICKEN PIE

1 chicken or chicken pieces (about 800 g)
250 ml chicken stock
bouquet garni
5 ml salt
freshly ground black pepper to taste
1 ml ground cloves
30 g margarine
1 onion, chopped
200 g mushrooms, halved
50 ml dry white wine
25 ml cake flour
150 g frozen peas
½ quantity Shortcrust Pastry (page 30) OR
½ quantity Puff Pastry (page 32)
beaten egg or milk to glaze

❶ Simmer chicken in stock with bouquet garni until cooked and tender.

❷ Remove chicken and bouquet garni from stock. Reserve liquid. Skin, debone and cut chicken meat into pieces. Add seasoning.

❸ Heat margarine in a heavy-based saucepan and sauté onion and mushrooms lightly.

❹ Heat cooking liquid and wine. Add chicken and mushrooms. Simmer about 15 minutes. Make a paste with flour, thicken sauce, and add peas.

❺ Spoon into a large ovenproof dish or four individual bowls.

❻ Roll out pastry thinly and cover chicken. Trim edges. Brush top with beaten egg or milk and bake in a preheated oven at 200 °C (400 °F) for 20 minutes.

Serves 4

TIPS

A bouquet garni is a bunch of herbs – normally a few parsley stalks, a sprig of thyme and a bayleaf – tied together with string or wrapped in muslin and then tied together. Place bundle in dish during cooking, and remove before serving.

Cut a lid for a single pie crust as follows: Invert the pie dish onto the rolled-out pastry and cut around the edge with a sharp knife.

Clockwise from top right: Vegetable Mix with Dumplings, Chicken Pie and Mince Roll.

SAVOURY MINCE DISH

BASE
100 g mashed potato
100 g butter or margarine
250 ml Snowflake cake flour (140 g)
5 ml baking powder
2 ml salt
1 egg, beaten

FILLING
250 g topside mince
20 ml cooking oil
1 onion, finely chopped
2 cloves garlic, crushed
150 ml sour cream
125 ml milk
3 eggs
250 ml grated Cheddar cheese (100 g)
15 ml chopped fresh parsley OR
5 ml dried
6 ml chopped fresh herbs OR
2 ml mixed dried herbs
3 ml salt
freshly ground black pepper to taste

❶ For base: Mix all ingredients. Press into base and sides of a greased 23 cm round pie dish.

❷ For filling: Fry mince in heated oil until colour changes. Add onion and garlic and sauté lightly.

❸ Beat sour cream, milk and eggs together. Add remaining ingredients and spoon into base.

❹ Bake in a preheated oven at 180 °C (350 °F) for 35 minutes.

Serves 4–6

VARIATION

BILTONG DISH

Substitute mince with 250 g grated biltong. Omit salt.

TIP

Fresh parsley can be quickly and neatly chopped in a cup or glass using a pair of sharp kitchen scissors.

FILLET PARCELS

4 slices beef fillet, 3 cm thick
3 ml salt
freshly ground black pepper to taste

FILLING
15 ml butter or margarine
1 onion, finely chopped
1 clove garlic, crushed
200 g mushrooms, chopped
3 ml salt
freshly ground black pepper to taste

1 quantity Cream Cheese Pastry (page 34)
beaten egg or milk to glaze

❶ Heat a griddle pan and brown fillet on both sides. Season, set aside on paper towel, and leave to cool slightly.

❷ For filling: Heat butter and sauté onion, garlic and mushrooms. Add seasoning and leave to cool.

❸ Roll out pastry to a thickness of 3 mm. Cut into squares large enough to accommodate fillet and filling. Place fillet in middle and top with filling.

❹ Bring four corners together and seal. Brush with beaten egg or milk.

❺ Place on a greased baking tray and bake in a preheated oven at 200 °C (400 °F) for 20–25 minutes.

Serves 4

TIP

A lean, tender cut of beef, fillet can be roasted whole or served as cuts.

BEEF STROGANOFF

25 ml cooking oil
25 ml margarine
1 kg topside, cut into strips
100 ml Snowflake cake flour (55 g)
1 onion, finely chopped
1 clove garlic, crushed
250 g mushrooms, halved
5 ml salt
freshly ground black pepper to taste
250 ml meat stock
250 ml sour cream

❶ Heat oil and margarine. Roll beef strips in flour and brown. Add onion and garlic, and sauté.

❷ Stir in mushrooms, salt and pepper and meat stock. Cover and simmer for approximately 30 minutes, until tender.

❸ Reduce heat, add sour cream, and simmer for a few minutes. Serve immediately.

Serves 4–6

VARIATION

For a low-calorie meal, substitute sour cream with low-fat plain yoghurt.

FISH IN BEER BATTER

250 ml Snowflake self-raising flour (140 g)
5 ml salt
15 ml chopped fresh herbs OR
5 ml mixed dried herbs
15 ml cooking oil
250 ml beer
extra flour for coating
800 g frozen hake fillets
cooking oil for frying

❶ Sift flour and salt. Add dried herbs, oil and beer.

❷ Coat fish with extra flour, dip into batter, and fry in shallow oil. Drain on paper towel.

❸ Serve with Tartare Sauce.

Tartare sauce

250 ml mayonnaise
2 eggs, hard-boiled and finely chopped
10 ml finely chopped gherkins, optional
2 spring onions, finely chopped
15 ml chopped fresh parsley OR
5 ml dried
15 ml chopped fresh tarragon OR
5 ml dried

Mix all ingredients together well, cover and chill in refrigerator until ready to serve.

Serves 4

SAVOURY PUMPKIN PIE

1 quantity Cream Cheese Pastry (page 34)

FILLING
15 ml butter
1 onion, finely chopped
3 rashers rindless streaky bacon, chopped
375 ml mashed, cooled pumpkin (340 g)
125 ml grated Cheddar cheese (50 g)
3 eggs
100 ml fresh milk OR cream
15 ml chopped fresh parsley OR
5 ml dried
2 ml salt
freshly ground black pepper to taste

❶ Press pastry into base and sides of a 23 cm ovenproof pie dish.

❷ For filling: Heat butter and sauté onion and bacon. Place in a bowl and cool slightly. Add pumpkin and cheese.

❸ Beat eggs and milk and add, with seasoning, to pumpkin mixture. Spoon onto base.

❹ Bake in a preheated oven at 180 °C (350 °F) for 45–50 minutes.

Serves 4–6

TIP

Drain pumpkin well before mashing.

Clockwise from top right: Fillet Parcels, Fish in Beer Batter and Savoury Pumpkin Pie.

CHEESE SOUFFLÉ

30 ml butter or margarine
30 ml Snowflake cake flour
250 ml milk
3 ml salt
freshly ground black pepper to taste
250 ml grated Cheddar cheese (100 g)
4 eggs, separated

❶ Melt butter in a saucepan. Add flour and stir over low heat for 1 minute. Remove from heat, add milk, and stir until smooth.

❷ Return to medium heat and stir continuously until boiling. Lower heat and cook for 3 minutes, stirring frequently. Add salt and pepper.

❸ Add grated cheese and stir until melted. Remove from heat. Beat egg yolks and add.

❹ Beat egg whites until soft peak stage and fold into cheese sauce.

❺ Spoon mixture into a medium-sized ungreased soufflé dish and place in a baking or roasting pan half-filled with water.

❻ Bake in a preheated oven at 180 °C (350 °F) for 40–50 minutes. Serve immediately.

Serves 2–4

VARIATIONS

BROCCOLI SOUFFLÉ

Substitute cheese by adding 500 ml cooked and drained broccoli florets to white sauce.

SWEETCORN SOUFFLÉ

Add 250 ml cream-style sweetcorn to basic white sauce.

TIP

Use greaseproof paper to prevent the soufflé from overflowing: cut a piece long enough to wrap around the dish. Fold it in half, lengthways, butter it to prevent the soufflé from sticking, and tie the paper around the dish with string. Remove carefully after baking.

CALZONE

This folded bread, filled with mozzarella cheese, is a delicious variation of a pizza.

1 quantity Pizza Dough (page 14)
100 g rump steak, cut into strips
20 ml cooking oil
1 onion, chopped
1 baby marrow, thinly sliced
1 carrot, cut julienne
250 ml grated mozzarella cheese (125 g) OR
Cheddar cheese (100 g)
1 ml salt
freshly ground black pepper to taste
6 ml chopped fresh origanum OR
2 ml dried
beaten egg or milk to glaze

❶ Follow recipe for pizza dough.

❷ After first rising, knock down and divide into two.

❸ Roll out two circles, each about 25 cm in diameter, and 3–5 mm thick.

❹ Brown meat in heated oil in a heavy-based saucepan. Add vegetables and stir-fry until cooked but still crisp. Add cheese and seasoning. Place filling onto one half of dough, leaving 2,5 cm free around border. Fold dough over and seal edges well.

❺ Place two calzones on a greased baking tray and brush with remaining oil. Cover with plastic wrap and leave to rise in a warm place for about 45 minutes until double in size.

❻ Brush with beaten egg or milk. Bake in a preheated oven at 200 °C (400 °F) for 15–20 minutes, or until golden brown. Serve hot.

Makes 2, depending on size

VARIATION

Substitute steak with any meat of your choice, such as ham or rindless bacon.

TUNA PIE

60 g margarine
60 ml Snowflake cake flour (35 g)
350 ml milk
2 ml salt
freshly ground black pepper to taste
2 x 200 g cans solid tuna in vegetable oil, drained and flaked
3 hard-boiled eggs, chopped
1 quantity Shortcrust Pastry (page 30)
beaten egg or milk to glaze

❶ Melt margarine and add flour to make a roux. Add hot milk and boil for a few minutes, stirring continuously until thick.

❷ Add salt, pepper, tuna and chopped eggs. Leave to cool slightly.

❸ Roll out pastry thinly. Line the bottom of a medium-sized, greased ovenproof dish with half of pastry. Fill with tuna filling and cover with remaining pastry. Decorate with pastry strips and brush with beaten egg or milk.

❹ Bake in a preheated oven at 200 °C (400 °F) for 20 minutes.

Serves 4

TIP

Canned tuna is always a good store cupboard item. It can be used in fish cakes, salads or pasta sauces.

From top: Cheese Soufflé and Calzone.

3

Pastries

Pastry is made from flour, fat and liquid, and can also include sugar, egg yolks, or other ingredients that enrich the pastry. These basic ingredients are the same for all kinds of pastry. Shortcrust pastry remains the most popular and versatile, while Puff pastry and flaky pastry take longer to make and are used in special dishes. Other pastries that are becoming more popular and are very versatile are cream cheese and soda-water pastry.

The method for making pastry will depend on the pastry being made, but a few important guidelines for obtaining success are generally applicable and should be followed for best results:

- When making a pastry using wholewheat flour it may be necessary to use less water as the wholewheat absorbs slightly less liquid.
- Always use cold ingredients and equipment, except when making Hot-water pastry. The water and fat used for making pastry should be ice cold.
- Use only butter, as it gives a better result than margarine.
- Use a sharp knife for cutting pastry if no pastry cutter is available.
- Work with your fingertips as they are the coolest part of the hand.
- The amount of liquid specified in a recipe is only a guideline; the amount needed will vary according to the moisture content of the flour used, and the humidity in the atmosphere. Too much liquid will cause the pastry to shrink.
- Do not stretch pastry during preparation as this will also cause shrinkage.
- It is important to work lightly with pastry as overhandling leads to shrinkage.
- Keep your work surface and rolling pin lightly floured. Use a dredger to ensure that the flour is spread evenly.
- If possible, roll pastry out on a marble surface as it is cold, smooth and hygienic.
- Never turn pastry over during rolling.
- Roll pastry in one direction only to maintain an even thickness.
- Leftover pastry should be rolled out and not bundled up.
- Chill pastry in tin before baking to prevent shrinkage in oven.
- Cooking time will depend on thickness and size of case.
- All pastries can be successfully frozen for up to 3 months if stored in an airtight container.
- If frozen, remove pastry from freezer 1 hour prior to use.

Lining a pastry flan

A pastry flan should be carefully lined. If stretched even slightly, the pastry will shrink when baked. After rolling out, lift the pastry gently, with the support of a rolling pin, and place it in the tin. Flour fingertips and press down lightly into base. Allow to stand for 30 minutes before baking.

Baking blind

This involves pre-baking the pastry case before adding the filling. Prick the base, place greaseproof paper over the pastry, and sprinkle with dried beans or peas. Bake according to the recipe, for about 10 minutes. Remove beans. (Store for later use.) Alternatively, use aluminium foil, with the shiny side upward. The foil will reflect the heat and prevent the pastry from rising, so the beans are not necessary in this instance. If the pastry case rises to a peak during baking, prick while still soft to allow air to escape.

Knocking up

This method is used to seal pastry edges, especially when making pies and tarts. To do this, brush one edge with water and press the two edges firmly together. Press lightly on the joined edges using a finger and a knife, gently knocking the edges of the pastry in order to seal them.

Decorating pastries

Your choice of decoration will depend on the type of pastry you are using, and on the size and shape of the dish. Whichever option you choose, start off by sealing the edges neatly.

- Pinch the edge using your forefinger and thumb, or press with a fork.
- Scallop the edge using the blunt edge of a knife.
- Make a fold on the edge of the pastry with your fingers.
- Plait pastry and place around edge.
- Make leaves, hearts, stars or fish. Brush with water and place on pastry.

Glazing

Glazing creates an attractive appearance. Glaze savoury dishes by brushing with beaten egg, or milk. Brush sweet pies with egg white; sprinkle with castor sugar.

TYPES OF PASTRY

Shortcrust pastry (Pâte Brisée)

To make shortcrust pastry, use one part fat to two parts flour. Handle the pastry quickly and lightly, using chilled ingredients. Once baked, pastry should be crisp with a fine, even texture. Shortcrust pastry becomes hard and tough for one of two reasons: if too much liquid is added, and when pastry is overhandled. Shortcrust pastry dishes include single crust pies, savoury flans, quiches and sweet flans. Remember: Keep ingredients cool, work quickly, and chill pastry before rolling out.

Successful pastry-making is easy to achieve by following the basic rules for baking blind, decorating and glazing.

Rich shortcrust pastry (Pâte Brisée à l'oeuf)

This pastry can be rolled out more thinly than basic shortcrust. Egg yolk and sugar are usually added, resulting in a richer pastry that will stay crisp for longer.

The butter and water used should be cold. Do not overwork the egg and butter, and chill the pastry for at least 30 minutes before rolling out. To line flan tin, lift pastry slightly and slide gently into tin, avoiding stretching. This pastry is ideal for making tartlet shells and is often baked blind.

Sweet flan pastry (Pâte Sucrée)

This pastry is similar to rich shortcrust pastry, with the addition of extra egg, sugar and vanilla essence, and needs a lot of kneading. Refrigerate for at least 30 minutes – a little longer, if possible – before rolling out.

Puff pastry (Pâte Feuilletée)

Its French name meaning 'leafy pastry', puff pastry has a texture that is delicate, very fine and flaky, and is ideal for making pie toppings, fine pastries, tarts, vol-au-vents and cocktail snacks.

An equal proportion of fat to flour is used to make this pastry. All ingredients should be well chilled while the pastry is being made and rolled out, and the pastry itself should be chilled a few times to ensure that the layers remain intact. A little lemon juice added to the water will further strengthen the layers.

The pastry rises as follows: the butter between the layers melts during baking and separates the layers, and the water present in the butter turns to steam, which causes the pastry to rise.

When making puff pastry it is essential to keep the ingredients and the work surface cool and to roll the pastry out evenly, without stretching it. Prepare the pastry a day in advance to allow it to rest.

Flaky pastry

This is not as delicate and soft as puff pastry, but it is flaky, rises high, and can be used for the same purposes. It is somewhat easier to make than puff pastry.

Hot-water pastry

The proportion used to make hot-water pastry is roughly one-third fat to flour. It is normally used to make raised pies in special oval, fluted metal pie moulds, and is also used for ham and game pies. Keep pastry warm during preparation and handle it quickly. However, chill before rolling out.

Cream cheese pastry

This rich pastry can be used for savoury or sweet dishes, and is very good if smooth cream cheese or cottage cheese is used. It is easy to handle if all the ingredients are cold. Chill well before rolling out.

Soda-water pastry

This is a good substitute for puff pastry as it also has a layered appearance, and is ideal for sweet or savoury dishes. All ingredients should be cold before use.

Choux pastry

This pastry differs from all other pastries because it is made in a saucepan, is soft and should be piped or spooned. When baked, it should be puffed, golden, dry and hollow inside.

For successful results, do not allow the water to boil before the butter has melted, so remove the pan from the heat as soon as the water starts boiling. Add flour all at once, return to heat, and mix until a ball forms. Add eggs one at a time to the slightly cooled mixture. Beat well after each addition.

Choux pastry should be baked until dry to ensure that it holds its shape. The secret, therefore, is to bake it in a very hot oven and then reduce the heat. Turn the stove off and leave the shells in the oven for 10 minutes to ensure that they dry out. After removing from the oven, pierce each shell to allow the steam to escape.

Fill shells an hour before serving or they will soften. Store empty shells in an airtight container. Heat for a few minutes to crisp up when needed, then fill.

The pastry can be kept in the refrigerator for one day if not needed immediately, or frozen, unbaked, for 3 months.

SHORTCRUST PASTRY

Shortcrust pastry is used for savoury dishes such as pies and pastries. It is suitable for freezing, though not for longer than 3 months.

500 ml Snowflake cake flour (280 g)
2 ml salt
125 g cold butter
125 ml iced water
5 ml lemon juice or brandy

❶ Sift flour and salt together.

❷ Cut butter into small pieces and rub into flour with fingertips until mixture resembles breadcrumbs.

❸ Mix water and lemon juice into dry ingredients to make a stiff dough. Knead well.

❹ Cover with plastic wrap and refrigerate for 1 hour. Roll out dough on floured surface to a thickness of 3 mm.

❺ Bake in a preheated oven at 200 °C (400 °F) for 20–25 minutes, or until golden brown.

Makes 2 flan cases

VARIATION

Substitute 250 ml cake flour with Snowflake Nutty Wheat.

TIP

The secret of success with this pastry is to avoid using too much liquid, which will make the pastry sticky, resulting in a dry crust. The pastry should be just moistened.

Shortcrust Pastry and Rich Shortcrust Pastry.

RICH SHORTCRUST PASTRY

Enriched by the addition of extra fat, sugar or egg yolk, this pastry is used for sweet and savoury dishes such as pies, pastries, tarts, tartlets or flans, and is also suitable for freezing. When using for savouries, omit the sugar.

500 ml Snowflake cake flour (280 g)
2 ml salt
190 g cold butter
15 ml castor sugar
1 egg yolk
20 ml iced water
5 ml lemon juice

❶ Sift flour and salt together.

❷ Cut butter into small pieces and rub into flour with fingertips until mixture resembles breadcrumbs.

❸ Add sugar if using. Mix egg yolk, water and lemon juice into dry ingredients to make a stiff dough. Knead well.

❹ Wrap dough in plastic wrap and chill in refrigerator for about 1 hour. Roll out on a floured surface to a thickness of 3 mm.

❺ Bake in a preheated oven at 200 °C (400 °F) for 20–25 minutes, or until golden brown.

Makes 2 flan cases

VARIATION

Substitute 250 ml cake flour with Snowflake Nutty Wheat.

FLAKY PASTRY

This pastry is not as delicate as puff pastry, but is flaky, rises high, and is easier to make than puff pastry. It has the same applications as puff pastry, namely pie toppings, cream horns and cocktail snacks.

500 ml Snowflake cake flour (280 g)
2 ml salt
150 g butter
125 ml iced water
5 ml lemon juice

❶ Sift flour and salt together.

❷ Cut butter into pea-sized pieces, add half to flour, and rub in until mixture resembles breadcrumbs.

❸ Mix iced water with lemon juice and cut in with a knife. Mix until smooth, forming a stiff dough.

❹ Flour surface and roll pastry to a thickness of 5 mm, keeping shape rectangular.

❺ Cover two-thirds of pastry with half of remaining butter.

❻ Fold the third of the pastry without butter to meet the other end piece. Fold in thirds again. Keep covered and chill for a while.

❼ Roll out and place remaining butter on two-thirds of pastry, then fold, turn and roll out. Refrigerate for at least 30 minutes.

❽ Bake in a preheated oven at 200 °C (400 °F) for 20–25 minutes, or until golden brown.

SODA-WATER PASTRY

This versatile pastry is delicate and is used for sweet and savoury dishes as well as small pastries such as sausage rolls and cream horns. It can be frozen for up to 3 months.

500 ml Snowflake cake flour (280 g)
3 ml salt
250 g cold butter
85 ml iced soda-water
15 ml lemon juice or brandy

❶ Sift flour and salt together. Rub in butter with fingertips until mixture resembles breadcrumbs.

❷ Add soda-water and lemon juice and mix to a stiff dough.

❸ Place in plastic wrap and refrigerate for 1 hour. Roll out dough on a floured surface to a thickness of 3 mm.

❹ Bake in a preheated oven at 200 °C (400 °F) for 20 minutes, or until golden brown.

PUFF PASTRY

500 ml Snowflake cake flour (280 g)
2 ml salt
250 g cold butter
125 ml iced water
5 ml lemon juice

❶ Sift flour and salt together. Roll butter into a flat, 15 cm square and keep chilled.

❷ Mix water with lemon juice, pour over flour, and cut in with a knife. Mix until smooth, forming a stiff dough.

❸ Flour surface and roll pastry to a thickness of 5 mm, keeping it rectangular.

❹ Place butter on centre of dough and fold corners to the middle to make an envelope, enclosing butter.

❺ Roll out pastry on a floured surface. Fold into three by turning bottom third up and top third down. Seal edges and chill.

❻ Repeat rolling and folding in three. Chill for 30 minutes.

❼ Repeat rolling and folding pastry seven times, chilling when necessary.

❽ Roll out and refrigerate for at least 30 minutes.

❾ Bake in a preheated oven at 200 °C (400 °F) for 20–25 minutes, or until golden brown.

TIP

Leftover pieces can be rolled out again for later use. Never form into a ball or the layers will be lost.

HOT-WATER PASTRY

Crisp and thicker than usual, this pastry is ideal for the bottom of pies and is frequently used for pastries.

125 ml boiling water
125 g butter or margarine
500 ml Snowflake self-raising flour (280 g)
2 ml salt

❶ Melt butter in hot water. Sift flour and salt together and mix with liquid until a soft dough is formed.

❷ Refrigerate for 1 hour to cool.

❸ On a floured surface, roll out dough to a thickness of 3 mm and bake in a preheated oven at 200 °C (400 °F) for 20 minutes, or until golden brown.

TIP

This is a soft pastry, which should be chilled well before using – at least 1 hour.

From top: Soda-water Pastry, Puff Pastry and Flaky Pastry.

CREAM CHEESE PASTRY

Cream cheese pastry is used for savoury dishes, small pastries and tartlets. It can be frozen for up to 3 months.

250 ml Snowflake cake flour (140 g)
2 ml salt
125 g cold butter
125 g smooth cottage cheese

❶ Sift flour and salt together. Rub in butter until mixture resembles breadcrumbs.

❷ Add cottage cheese and mix to a soft dough.

❸ Place in plastic wrap and refrigerate for a few hours. On a floured surface, roll out dough to a thickness of 3 mm.

❹ Bake in a preheated oven at 180 °C (350 °F) for 25–30 minutes.

VARIATION

Substitute half of the cake flour with wholewheat flour.

TIPS

To make the pastry easier to work, be sure to have the butter and cottage cheese cold. As it is a soft pastry it should be chilled before using.

If pastry has been left overnight in the refrigerator, allow to stand at room temperature for at least 1 hour before rolling out.

SWEET FLAN PASTRY

This pastry is used to make delicate sweet tarts. It can be frozen for up to 3 months.

250 ml Snowflake cake flour (140 g)
2 ml salt
65 ml castor sugar (55 g)
60 g butter
2 egg yolks
2 ml vanilla essence

❶ Sift flour and salt together. Add sugar and rub in butter with fingertips until the mixture resembles breadcrumbs.

❷ Add egg yolks and essence and work into a firm dough. Knead pastry well until smooth.

❸ On a floured surface, roll out dough to a thickness of 3 mm. Line a greased, 24 cm loose-bottomed flan tin.

❹ Cover with plastic wrap; refrigerate for 1 hour. Prick base and bake blind in a preheated oven at 190 °C (375 °F) for 10 minutes. Remove paper and beans, then bake a further 5 minutes until pastry is golden brown.

❺ Allow to cool in pan before turning out onto wire rack to cool completely.

Makes one flan case or 12 medium tartlets

VARIATION

Substitute half the flour with Snowflake Nutty Wheat.

TIP

The food processor is ideal for making this pastry as it needs to be worked thoroughly into a very fine and crisp pastry.

CHOUX PASTRY

This pastry is used for sweet and savoury profiteroles (cream puffs), éclairs or gâteaux. Like other kinds of pastry, it freezes successfully.

125 ml water
65 g butter
125 ml Snowflake cake flour (70 g)
1 ml salt
2 eggs

❶ Place water and butter in a saucepan. Bring slowly to the boil, allowing butter to melt before water boils.

❷ Remove from heat; add flour and salt. Return to heat and stir quickly until a ball forms in the middle, and the dough comes away from the sides.

❸ Remove from heat and leave to cool for about 5 minutes.

❹ Add eggs one at a time, beating well after each addition until dough is stiff.

❺ If making puffs, place teaspoonfuls on greased baking tray or pipe in long shapes for éclairs.

❻ Bake in a preheated oven at 200 °C (400 °F) for 10 minutes.

❼ Reduce heat to 180 °C (350 °F) for 15 minutes. Leave to cool in oven.

❽ Fill with cream, Confectioner's Custard (page 43) or savoury fillings.

Makes 16 puffs or 12 éclairs

TIPS

Raw dough can be kept, covered, in a cool place for 1 day or frozen for 3 months.

Store empty shells in an airtight container. When needed, reheat for a few minutes to make crisp.

From top: Choux Pastry, Sweet Flan Pastry and Cream Cheese Pastry.

TEATIME TREATS AND TARTS

WHEN CONSIDERING WHAT TO MAKE FOR TEA, BEAR IN MIND FACTORS LIKE THE AGE OF THE GUESTS AND THE SEASON. SWEET FRUIT TARTS ARE USUALLY A HIT, BUT THE SEASON WILL, TO A LARGE DEGREE, DETERMINE WHAT YOU MAKE. OLD FAVOURITES LIKE SCONES, DOUGHNUTS AND CRUMPETS ARE ALSO IDEAL FOR TEA. FOR SUCCESSFUL TEA PARTIES IT IS ESSENTIAL TO MASTER THE ART OF MAKING RICH SHORTCRUST PASTRY AND SWEET FLAN PASTRY, WHICH WILL EQUIP YOU FOR PREPARING DELICIOUS TARTS OR TARTLETS WITH FILLINGS.

SCONES

500 ml Snowflake cake flour (280 g)
15 ml baking powder
2 ml salt
75 ml castor sugar (60 g)
65 g margarine or butter
1 egg
125 ml milk

❶ Sift dry ingredients together. Add sugar.

❷ Rub margarine into dry ingredients until mixture resembles breadcrumbs. Mix egg and milk together and add to dry ingredients, forming a soft, but not sticky, dough.

❸ Turn out onto a floured surface and pat out lightly, to a thickness of 20 mm. Cut into rounds or squares. Place on a greased baking tray and bake in a preheated oven at 200 °C (400 °F) for 12–15 minutes.

❹ Serve scones with honey, syrup or jam and cream.

Makes about 8, depending on size

VARIATIONS

CHEESE SCONES

Omit sugar and add 250 ml grated Cheddar cheese to dry ingredients.

Use celery salt instead of plain salt and omit sugar.

Omit sugar from dough. Pat out and spread with cheese spread, fish paste, sandwich spread or pâté. Roll up dough as for a Swiss roll and cut into 2,5 cm slices. Arrange cut side up on baking trays; bake as usual.

TIP

For delicious, light scones, use half milk and half water.

WHOLEWHEAT SCONES

1 egg
65 ml cooking oil
about 150 ml milk
250 ml Snowflake cake flour (140 g)
250 ml Snowflake Nutty Wheat (150 g)
20 ml baking powder
2 ml salt

❶ Beat egg lightly with a fork in a 250 ml cup, add oil, and fill with milk to 250 ml measure.

❷ Sift dry ingredients together. Add bran left behind in sieve.

❸ Make a well in the centre and mix in the liquid. Mix to a soft dough.

❹ Turn out onto a floured surface, pat lightly to a thickness of 2 cm and cut into rounds with a scone cutter.

❺ Place scones on a greased baking tray and bake in a preheated oven at 220 °C (425 °F) for 10–15 minutes.

Makes about 8, depending on size

VARIATIONS

FRUIT SCONES

Add 125 ml fruit cake mix or 50 g chopped, stewed fruit, and 15 ml castor sugar to dry ingredients.

CHEESE SCONES

Add 250 ml grated Cheddar cheese and 1 ml cayenne pepper to whole-wheat scone recipe.

For breakfast, make one large scone.

TIP

Freeze scones for up to 6 months in an airtight container or wrapping.

CRUMPETS

250 ml Snowflake cake flour (140 g)
10 ml baking powder
1 ml salt
30 ml sugar
1 egg
200 ml milk
15 ml margarine, melted

❶ Sift flour, baking powder and salt together. Add sugar.

❷ Beat the egg, milk and melted margarine together and add to dry ingredients.

❸ Beat until smooth and leave to stand for 30 minutes.

❹ Fry spoonfuls of batter on a hot, greased griddle or frying pan.

❺ Fry until golden brown, turning when bubbles appear on surface.

❻ Serve with butter, jam or honey.

Makes 12–15

TIPS

After removing crumpets from griddle, place on a clean, dry dishcloth to keep soft.

Freeze crumpets on top of one another, wrapping a few together in plastic wrap. Keep in deep-freeze for up to 2 months.

From top: Wholewheat Scones and Scones.

CHEESY BROWN CRUMPETS

375 ml Snowflake brown bread meal (210 g)
10 ml baking powder
1 ml salt
250 ml grated Cheddar cheese (100 g)
125 ml cooking oil
125 ml milk
3 eggs
50 ml sugar (40 g)

❶ Sift brown bread meal, baking powder and salt together, and add cheese. Add bran left behind in sieve.

❷ Beat oil, milk, eggs and sugar together until sugar has dissolved. Mix with dry ingredients to form a smooth batter.

❸ Allow to stand for 30 minutes before frying spoonfuls on a hot, greased griddle or in a frying pan. When bubbles appear on surface, turn crumpets and allow to fry on the other side. Repeat until all the batter has been used.

❹ Serve hot with butter or margarine.

Makes 20

TIP

Always mix liquid into flour, and not the other way around. If lumps form, rub mixture through a sieve. Batter should have the consistency of thin cream.

DOUGHNUTS

500 ml Snowflake cake flour (280 g)
5 ml salt
8 ml instant dry yeast (5 g)
30 ml butter or margarine
1 egg, beaten
150 ml warm milk
smooth apricot jam
cooking oil for frying
castor sugar

❶ Sift the flour and salt together and add yeast.

❷ Rub in butter until mixture resembles fine breadcrumbs.

❸ Combine egg and milk. Add to dry ingredients, mixing to a soft dough.

❹ Knead for about 10 minutes, until dough is smooth and elastic.

❺ Place dough in an oiled bowl, cover, and allow to rest for about 30 minutes.

❻ Knock down and divide into 12 pieces.

❼ Roll into balls and make a hole in the middle of each with your finger. Fill with about one teaspoon jam and pinch closed.

❽ Cover with oiled plastic wrap and allow to rise in a warm place until double in size – about 20 minutes.

❾ Deep-fry in hot oil until golden brown.

❿ Drain on paper towel and toss in castor sugar.

Makes 20

VARIATION

Fry the doughnuts first, make a hole in the centre of each with your finger, and then fill with jam.

TIP

To make ring doughnuts, cut out rounds from centre. Fry small rounds, too, and coat both with glacé icing or melted chocolate.

WAFFLES

375 ml Snowflake cake flour (210 g)
15 ml baking powder
2 ml salt
15 ml sugar
300 ml milk
2 eggs, separated
50 g butter, melted, or cooking oil

❶ Sift dry ingredients. Add sugar.

❷ Whisk milk, egg yolks and melted butter together. Add to dry ingredients, mixing until smooth.

❸ Fold in beaten egg whites and leave batter to stand for 30 minutes.

❹ Bake in a hot waffle pan until waffle is golden brown. Serve warm with syrup, honey or caramel sauce.

Makes 6 waffles, depending on size

TIP

If the waffle pan is too cold the waffles will stick, or be spotted. A moderately hot temperature is ideal and has been reached when a few drops of cold water sprinkled on the heated grid form bouncy white balls.

Caramel sauce

250 ml brown sugar (200 g)
50 g butter
250 ml milk
25 ml custard powder
1 ml salt
5 ml caramel essence

❶ Caramelize brown sugar and butter slightly until they start to brown.

❷ Remove from heat; gradually add 200 ml heated milk. Stir to dissolve sugar.

❸ Mix custard powder, salt and remaining milk to a smooth paste.

❹ Add to milk and bring to boil until thick, then cook for about 3 minutes. Remove from heat and add essence.

TIP

For a thicker sauce, add more custard powder.

From top: Doughnuts, Cheesy Brown Crumpets and Waffles.

STRAWBERRY CHIFFON TART

15 ml gelatine
65 ml cold water
2 eggs, separated
15 ml lemon juice
125 ml castor sugar (105 g)
250 ml crushed fresh strawberries

1 quantity Sweet Flan Pastry, baked (page 34)

❶ Soak gelatine in the cold water and dissolve over hot water.

❷ Beat egg yolks slightly, add lemon juice and 100 ml of sugar. Cook in top of double boiler over simmering water, stirring constantly until thickened.

❸ Remove from heat and stir in gelatine until dissolved. Add strawberries and chill mixture until it starts to thicken.

❹ Beat egg whites with remaining sugar until soft peak stage. Fold into strawberry mixture.

❺ Fill pastry shell, chill until set, and garnish with strawberries and whipped cream.

> TIPS
>
> *Beat egg whites until they are stiff, but not too dry.*
>
> *To test whether the gelatine has begun to set, place a spoon into the mixture, and then remove the spoon. If the gelatine has started to set, the mixture should stay apart for a few seconds.*

PUFFY APPLE RINGS

250 ml Snowflake self-raising flour (140 g)
2 ml salt
1 egg, separated
200 ml milk
3 apples, peeled and cored
cooking oil for frying
cinnamon sugar

❶ Sift flour and salt together. Beat in egg yolk and milk until smooth.

❷ Beat egg white until soft peak stage and fold gently into batter.

❸ Slice apples into rings (about 5 mm thick), cover with batter and deep-fry in hot oil.

❹ Drain apple rings on paper towel and sprinkle with cinnamon sugar. Eat immediately as they become soggy quickly.

Makes about 15

> TIP
>
> *Cooking oil is ready for frying when it turns a cube of bread pale brown in about 45 seconds.*

LEMON MERINGUE PIE

397 g can condensed milk
125 ml lemon juice
5 ml grated lemon rind
2 eggs, separated
1quantity Sweet Flan Pastry, baked (page 34)
25 ml castor sugar

❶ Combine condensed milk, lemon juice, lemon rind and egg yolks and mix well until smooth.

❷ Spoon into baked pastry shell.

❸ Beat egg whites and gradually add castor sugar while beating, until soft peak stage.

❹ Cover filling with meringue and bake in a preheated oven at 180 °C (350 °F) for about 10 minutes, or until golden brown. Remember that meringue burns easily.

> TIPS
>
> *One average lemon yields about 40 ml juice.*
>
> *Cut a meringue neatly using a knife blade that has been lightly coated in cooking oil.*

BANANA FRITTERS

250 ml Snowflake cake flour (140 g)
10 ml baking powder
15 ml cornflour
2 ml salt
1 egg
125 ml milk
50 ml sugar (40 g)
15 ml cooking oil
4 bananas, halved and then quartered
cooking oil for frying
cinnamon
castor sugar

❶ Sift cake flour, baking powder, cornflour and salt together.

❷ Whisk egg, milk, sugar and oil together and add to dry ingredients. Mix until smooth and leave to stand for 30 minutes.

❸ Dip banana pieces into batter and deep fry in hot oil until golden brown.

❹ Drain on paper towel and sprinkle with cinnamon and castor sugar.

Makes 16

VARIATION

Substitute banana with any other fruit, such as pineapple or cherries.

> TIPS
>
> *Squeeze lemon juice over raw, peeled apples or bananas to prevent discoloration.*
>
> *To deep-fry fritters, use an electric fryer, deep-frying pan or deep, wide saucepan. Pour in cooking oil to a depth of at least 8 cm.*
>
> *To shallow-fry fritters, use a heavy frying pan and pour in cooking oil to a depth of not more than 5 mm.*

From top: Strawberry Chiffon Pie, Puffy Apple Rings, Banana Fritters and Lemon Meringue Pie.

APPLE TART

FILLING
3 large green apples, peeled, cored and sliced OR 385 g can pie apples
125 ml sugar (100 g)
125 ml raisins (75 g)
5 ml ground cinnamon
4 cloves
20 ml lemon juice

BASE AND CRUST
125 g margarine
125 ml castor sugar (105 g)
1 egg
500 ml Snowflake cake flour (280 g)
10 ml baking powder
2 ml salt

❶ For filling: Mix apple slices with other filling ingredients in a saucepan.

❷ Simmer for about 5 minutes. Drain off excess juice and leave to cool. Remove cloves.

❸ For base and crust: Beat margarine and sugar together. Add egg and beat until light and fluffy.

❹ Sift dry ingredients and add to egg mixture, forming a soft dough.

❺ Press half of dough into a greased 23 cm pie dish. Spoon apple filling onto pastry.

❻ Coarsely grate remaining dough over filling.

❼ Bake in a preheated oven at 160 °C (325 °F) for 1 hour.

❽ Dust with icing sugar and serve hot or cold with cream.

TIP

To prevent a soggy base, sprinkle bottom of pastry with a mixture of flour and sugar before placing fruit on top.

FRUIT CUSTARD TARTLETS

1 quantity Sweet Flan Pastry (page 34) OR Rich Shortcrust Pastry (page 31) baked blind in small pastry tins

FILLING
250 ml milk
50 ml castor sugar (40 g)
50 ml cornflour (25 g)
1 ml salt
1 egg
5 ml vanilla essence or lemon juice
250 ml fresh cream, whipped

TOPPING
500 g fresh fruit such as strawberries, sliced bananas, pitted cherries, mandarin segments, sliced peaches, skinned grapes, blueberries, gooseberries, sliced pawpaw

GLAZE
125 ml smooth apricot jam (165 g)
15 ml water, brandy or lemon juice

❶ For filling: Heat milk in a saucepan. Mix sugar, cornflour and salt with a little of the milk. Add to remaining milk and bring to boil, stirring constantly until mixture starts to thicken.

❷ Beat egg slightly. Add some of warm mixture and return to saucepan; cook for a few minutes while beating to prevent lumps from forming.

❸ Cool, add essence and whipped cream. Fill tartlet cases.

❹ For topping: Arrange fruit on filling.

❺ For glaze: Heat ingredients together, stirring until smooth. Brush fruit with warm glaze.

Makes 12–15, depending on size

VARIATION

PASSION FRUIT TARTLETS

Fill pastry tartlets with custard, but substitute fruit topping with passion fruit sauce:

115 g can granadilla pulp
10 ml lemon juice
500 ml icing sugar (250 g)
Mix all ingredients until smooth.

BRANDY SNAPS

125 g butter
125 ml sugar (100 g)
125 ml golden syrup
250 ml Snowflake cake flour (140 g)
2 ml salt
5 ml ground ginger
15 ml brandy
500 ml fresh cream, whipped

❶ Place butter, sugar and syrup in a heavy-based saucepan; stir over moderate heat until sugar has dissolved. Remove from heat and cool slightly.

❷ Stir flour, salt and ginger into mixture. Stir well and add brandy.

❸ Drop teaspoonfuls of mixture onto greased baking tray, allowing enough space for spreading.

❹ Bake in a preheated oven at 180 °C (350 °F) for 10–12 minutes. Remove with buttered spatula and roll around the greased handle of a wooden spoon. Leave a few minutes until biscuit firms.

❺ Store in an airtight container for a few days and fill with whipped cream, spooned or piped in.

Makes 40

VARIATION

Cool brandy snaps flat; serve layered with whipped cream and strawberries.

TIPS

Use the entire blade of the spatula and not only the point to lift the freshly cooked brandy snaps.

Do not bake longer than 10–12 minutes or snaps will be tough, not crisp.

After baking: Turn off the heat and open the oven door, leaving the biscuits in the oven to keep warm while you work. If allowed to cool they will become hard and brittle and impossible to shape – so work quickly! If biscuits begin hardening before moulding, return to oven at 140 °C for a minute or two until they soften.

From top: Apple Tart, Brandy Snaps, Fruit Custard Tartlets and Custard Slice.

CUSTARD SLICES

CONFECTIONER'S CUSTARD
375 ml milk
75 ml sugar (60 g)
30 ml Snowflake cake flour
20 ml cornflour
2 eggs
2 egg yolks
2 ml vanilla essence

1 quantity Puff Pastry (page 32) OR
1 quantity Flaky Pastry (page 32)
Glacé Icing (page 67)

❶ Bring 300 ml milk to the boil. Mix sugar, flour and cornflour with remaining milk.

❷ Add hot milk to flour paste. Beat eggs and egg yolks and gradually add to the warm mixture.

❸ Return to stove and cook over low heat, stirring constantly until thickened. Leave to cool before adding vanilla essence.

❹ Roll pastry into a large rectangle; cut into 10 cm x 5 cm rectangles. Bake in a preheated oven at 200 °C (400 °F) for 15 minutes, until golden brown.

❺ Spread custard on half of the pastry pieces. Place remaining pastry pieces on top and decorate with Glacé Icing (page 67).

Makes 16–20

VARIATION

Sandwich the pastry slices together with strawberry jam and cream.

TIP

Keep refrigerated for up to 2 days.

CREAM PUFFS

1 quantity Choux Pastry (page 34)
fresh cream, beaten
cooking chocolate, melted OR
icing sugar

❶ To make puffs, place teaspoonfuls of pastry on greased baking tray.

❷ Bake in a preheated oven at 200 °C (400 °F) for 10 minutes and reduce to 180 °C (350 °F) for 15 minutes.

❸ When cool, fill with cream and top with melted chocolate or dust with icing sugar. Alternatively, fill with Lemon Filling, Ham and Cheese Filling or Custard Filling (all this page).

Makes 16

VARIATIONS

ÉCLAIRS

Spoon choux pastry into a piping bag and pipe onto éclair tin. Spoon melted chocolate or Chocolate Glacé Icing (page 58) over baked éclair, once cool.

Makes 12

Savoury puffs are made a little smaller. Fill just before serving or pastry will become soft.

For a quick dessert: fill puffs with spoonfuls of cream or ice-cream and pour hot, melted chocolate over. To melt chocolate: Chocolate should never be melted over direct heat or come into contact with water. Instead, use a double boiler, placing the chocolate in a pot over boiling water. The water in the bottom pot should not touch the base of the top saucepan. Bring the water to the boil, stirring chocolate until smooth. For melting chocolate in the microwave, set power on high or 100 % for 2–3 minutes; cook until chocolate has melted, stirring once.

Lemon filling

125 ml boiling water
5 ml grated lemon rind
100 ml sugar (80 g)
30 ml cornflour
1 egg, beaten
50 ml lemon juice
15 ml margarine

❶ Mix boiling water and lemon rind together.

❷ Add to dry ingredients in a saucepan. Boil until mixture has thickened.

❸ Pour some of the hot mixture onto beaten egg, then add this to rest of hot mixture. Add lemon juice and margarine.

Ham and cheese filling

30 ml margarine
30 ml Snowflake cake flour
250 ml milk
2 ml salt
1 ml cayenne pepper
15 ml chopped fresh parsley OR
5 ml dried
200 ml chopped smoked ham (100 g)
250 ml grated Cheddar cheese (100 g)

❶ Heat margarine in a saucepan and add flour. Add hot milk and stir constantly while cooking until thickened. Add salt, cayenne pepper and parsley.

❷ Add ham and cheese and leave mixture to cool before using.

Custard filling

125 ml Snowflake cake flour (70 g)
125 ml sugar (100 g)
2 ml salt
500 ml milk
2 eggs, beaten
10 ml butter
5 ml vanilla essence

❶ Mix flour, sugar and salt in the top of a double boiler. Add milk and beat until smooth.

❷ Pour a little hot milk mixture into beaten eggs; add this to rest of hot mixture.

❸ Beat while cooking until thickened, – about 3 minutes. Remove from heat and add butter and essence.
Leave to cool.

VARIATION

Substitute vanilla essence with lemon essence.

CREAM HORNS

1 quantity Puff Pastry (page 32) OR
Flaky Pastry (page 32)
1 egg white, beaten
60 ml strawberry jam
125 ml fresh cream

❶ Roll out pastry into a rectangular shape, to a thickness of 3 mm. Cut into strips 2,5 cm wide. Brush these lightly with beaten egg white.

❷ Grease cream horn moulds and, with damp side inwards, turn strips around greased moulds, starting at the pointed end of the mould and making sure that the strips overlap.

❸ Brush with egg white and place on a greased baking tray.

❹ Bake in a preheated oven at 220 °C (425 °F) for 8–10 minutes, until crisp and golden brown. Allow to cool.

❺ Place 5 ml jam inside and fill with beaten cream.

Makes 12

TIP

Pastry horns lose their crispness very quickly. To ensure crispness, do not make horns more than 2 hours before needed. Fill at the last minute.

From top: *Puffs with Ham and Cheese Filling and Cream Horns.*

BASIC FLAN

65 g butter
125 ml milk
2 eggs
200 ml sugar (160 g)
375 ml Snowflake cake flour (210 g)
10 ml baking powder
1 ml salt

❶ Heat butter and milk together until butter has melted.

❷ Beat eggs and sugar until light and fluffy.

❸ Sift dry ingredients and fold into egg mixture, together with milk. Beat slightly until smooth.

❹ Pour into two greased, fancy 24 cm flan tins. Bake in a preheated oven at 180 °C (350 °F) for 15–20 minutes.

❺ Leave flans in tins for a few minutes before turning onto a wire rack to cool.

❻ Fill with Ginger Filling, Gooseberry and Orange Filling or Pineapple Filling (all this page).

Makes 2 flans

TIP

If kept airtight, flans can be successfully frozen for 4–5 months.

Ginger filling

250 ml water
250 ml golden syrup
50 ml custard powder (25 g)
2 ml ground ginger
whipped cream for decorating

❶ Bring 200 ml water and the syrup to boil. Dissolve custard powder in remaining water.

❷ Pour warm syrup into custard powder, add ginger and pour back into saucepan.

❸ Boil until thickened – about 3 minutes.

❹ Leave to cool slightly and then pour into flan.

❺ When set, decorate with cream.

Gooseberry and orange filling

410 g can gooseberries in syrup
125 ml golden syrup
100 ml orange juice
50 ml custard powder (25 g)
5 ml grated orange rind
whipped cream for decorating

❶ Drain gooseberries and pour syrup into saucepan. Bring to boil.

❷ Stir in golden syrup and reheat until boiling.

❸ Mix orange juice and custard powder together to a smooth paste. Stir into syrup mixture. Cook until mixture is smooth and thickened.

❹ Add gooseberries and rind. Leave mixture to cool slightly, then pour into flan. Chill in refrigerator for a while to set.

❺ Decorate with cream.

Pineapple filling

15 ml margarine
200 ml sugar (160 g)
1 egg, separated
25 ml cornflour
250 ml crushed pineapple
2 ml salt
2 ml vanilla essence
125 ml fresh cream, whipped

❶ Cook margarine, sugar, egg yolk, cornflour and pineapple together until thickened.

❷ Add salt, vanilla essence, beaten egg white and whipped cream. Leave mixture to cool before filling prepared flan case.

CRUSTLESS MILK TART

30 ml butter
4 eggs, separated
250 ml castor sugar (210 g)
250 ml Snowflake cake flour (140 g)
5 ml baking powder
1 ml salt
1 litre milk
5 ml vanilla essence
ground cinnamon

❶ Melt butter. Add egg yolks and castor sugar, and beat well.

❷ Sift dry ingredients together and add to egg yolk mixture.

❸ Beat in milk and essence. Fold in beaten egg whites, then pour mixture into a greased 22 cm x 33 cm ovenproof tart dish.

❹ Sprinkle with cinnamon and bake in a preheated oven at 160 °C (325 °F) for 55–60 minutes.

TIP

To separate the yolk of an egg from the white, break the egg into a saucer, upturn a small glass over the yolk, and pour off the white.

PECAN PIE

½ quantity Rich Shortcrust Pastry (page 31)
300 ml pecan nuts (125 g)
60 g butter, melted
200 ml brown sugar (160 g)
3 eggs, beaten
100 ml golden syrup
5 ml vanilla essence

❶ Roll out pastry and line a greased 23 cm pie dish. Bake blind in a preheated oven at 180 °C (350 °F) for 10 minutes. Remove paper and beans.

❷ Arrange pecan nuts over partially cooked pastry case.

❸ Lightly beat melted butter, sugar and eggs together. Add syrup while beating until foamy. Add essence.

❹ Pour egg mixture over nuts. Bake in a preheated oven at 180 °C (350 °F) for 40–45 minutes. Leave to set.

❺ Serve hot or cold with whipped cream or ice cream.

TIP

After baking, pie will not be quite set, but will set once slightly cooled.

From top: Pecan Pie and Basic Flan with Gooseberry and Orange Filling.

5

CAKES

A BIRTHDAY PARTY OR SPECIAL TEA PARTY IS INCOMPLETE WITHOUT A CAKE. INCLUDING SOMETHING FOR EVERY OCCASION, THIS CHAPTER OFFERS A DELICIOUS SELECTION OF OLD FAVOURITES AND NEW IDEAS THAT WILL SUIT A VARIETY OF TASTES – AND BUDGETS!

PLAIN CAKES CAN BE TRANSFORMED INTO SPECIAL TREATS WITH FILLINGS OR TOPPINGS TO SUIT THE OCCASION. EXPERIENCED AND INEXPERIENCED BAKERS ALIKE WILL HAVE GREAT SUCCESS WITH ANY OF THESE IRRESISTIBLE CAKES.

GUIDELINES FOR BAKING CAKES

Preparing and mixing

To ensure success when baking cakes it is essential to weigh and measure accurately, and to follow the recipe carefully. Use the minimum amount of liquid, as more can always be added if necessary.

Using an electric beater is much easier and quicker than beating by hand. Start on low speed and, once the ingredients are combined, increase speed. Avoid overbeating as this breaks down the air bubbles that have formed in the mixture.

Bake the cake as soon after mixing as possible, as after standing too long, it may not rise as it should. Bang tin slightly before baking to remove air bubbles.

It is important to use the recommended tin size as the baking time will be different for other tin sizes. Baking times provided in the recipes are approximate, however, because many factors may influence the time required.

All of the recipes in this book have been tested in a conventional oven; a microwave oven was not used. For baking, conventional ovens produce better results.

Greasing cake tins

Most cake tins – even the 'non-stick' ones – need greasing. This can be done by brushing or spreading shortening over the inside of the tin, or by spraying.

Lining cake tins

For cakes that are moist and break easily, it will be necessary to line the tin. Heavy fruit cakes need a few layers of lining to prevent the cake from browning too much.

Use the base of the tin as a guideline for cutting out a circle of greaseproof paper. The circle should be 5 cm wider all round as it should be snipped at intervals. The lining for the sides should also be cut 5 cm wider. Place the lining for the sides in the tin first, and thereafter the base lining.

Flouring cake tins

Flour is sometimes dusted lightly on the inside of the tin after greasing to give extra protection against sticking. Sprinkle flour sparingly over the greased surface, and remove excess.

Testing cakes

Only start testing whether your cake is done after three-quarters of the baking time has been completed, using one of the following methods:

- Press the top of the cake lightly. If the cake is done it will spring back, and no impression will be left. This is a good way of testing if lighter cakes are done.

- Insert a fine skewer into the centre of the cake, then remove. If the cake is cooked, no cake mixture should stick to the skewer.

- When done, the cake will come away from the sides of the tin.

Cooling

Allow cakes to settle in the tin for 5–10 minutes before turning out and cooling on a wire rack. Air can then circulate and prevent the cake from becoming soggy.

To prevent wire rack marks from forming on the cake during cooling, place a clean tea towel on the rack before turning the cake onto it. Do not ice cakes until they are completely cold.

Storing

Cakes are best stored in an airtight container in a cool place. A piece of apple placed in the container helps to keep cakes moist.

Cream cakes or vegetable cakes should be stored in the refrigerator. Store sponge cakes and quick mixes for 2–4 days; rich fruit cakes 4–6 months.

Freezing

Unfilled and undecorated cakes freeze well for 3–6 months. Cakes can be frozen while still slightly warm to ensure greater freshness after defrosting.

To freeze, wrap cake in plastic wrap or heavy foil, making sure that it is airtight, and freeze as quickly as possible to prevent the formation of ice crystals.

Sometimes it is more convenient to freeze cakes once filled and iced. The best fillings and icings for freezing are those with a high shortening content. Water icing will be brittle on thawing. Place iced cake in the freezer, uncovered, until firm. Remove from freezer, wrap and seal, then return to freezer. Iced cakes freeze well for up to 3 months.

Defrosting

Allow undecorated cakes to defrost at room temperature for 1–2 hours, depending on size, and then fill and decorate. Decorated cakes should be thawed in the refrigerator overnight. Defrosting can also be done in the microwave, but the cake will become stale more quickly.

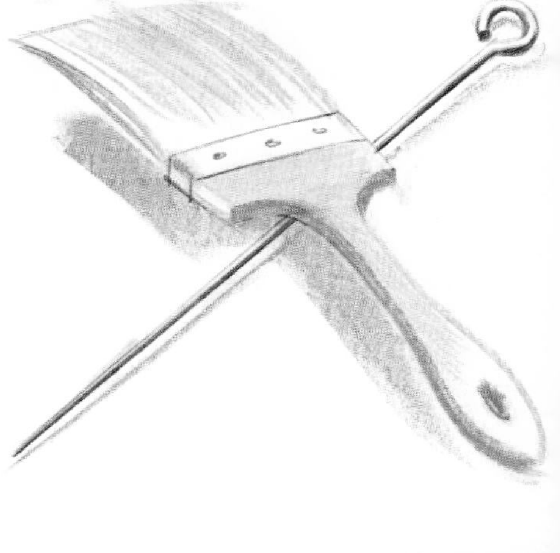

Many recipes can be turned into wonderful cakes by following basic guidelines on greasing, lining, resting and cooling cakes.

CARROT AND BANANA CAKE

125 ml brown sugar (100 g)
2 eggs
125 ml cooking oil
250 ml Snowflake white bread flour (140 g)
10 ml baking powder
5 ml bicarbonate of soda
250 ml finely grated carrot (125 g)
3 large bananas, mashed (250 ml)
125 ml seedless raisins OR sultanas (75 g)
icing sugar

❶ Whisk sugar, eggs and oil together.

❷ Sift dry ingredients and add, alternately with carrot, bananas and raisins, to egg mixture.

❸ Pour into a greased 22 cm ring cake tin. Bake in a preheated oven at 180 °C (350 °F) for 35–40 minutes.

❹ Leave in tin for a few minutes before turning onto a wire rack to cool. Dust with icing sugar.

TIP

If baked in a ring tin, the cake will be much easier to slice and serve.

NUTTY CHERRY CAKE

125 g margarine
125 ml brown sugar (100 g)
2 eggs, separated
375 ml Snowflake cake flour (210 g)
2 ml salt
5 ml baking powder
100 ml milk

TOPPING
250 ml halved glacé cherries (150 g)
250 ml chopped pecan nuts (100 g)
75 ml icing sugar (40 g)

❶ Beat margarine and sugar together until light and creamy.

❷ Add egg yolks one at a time, beating well after each addition.

❸ Sift dry ingredients and add alternately with milk to creamed egg mixture.

❹ Spread batter into a greased, loose-bottomed 20 cm round cake tin.

❺ For topping: Beat egg whites until soft peak stage.

❻ Fold cherries, nuts and icing sugar into egg whites.

❼ Spread on top of batter and bake in a preheated oven at 160 °C (325 °F) for 1¼ hours.

TIPS

If you notice that the meringue is browning too quickly while the cake is baking, reduce the oven temperature.

Do not turn cake out to cool; instead, remove from loose-bottomed cake tin and place on cooling rack.

CHOCOLATE OIL CAKE

4 eggs
250 ml sugar (200 g)
375 ml Snowflake cake flour (210 g)
50 ml cocoa powder
15 ml baking powder
2 ml salt
125 ml boiling water
125 ml cooking oil

CHOCOLATE BUTTER ICING
125 g butter
375 ml icing sugar (200 g)
30 ml cocoa powder
5 ml vanilla essence

❶ Whisk the eggs and sugar together until light and fluffy.

❷ Sift dry ingredients and gently fold into mixture, with water and oil.

❸ Turn into two lined, greased 20 cm cake tins and bake in a preheated oven at 180 °C (350 °F) for 20–25 minutes. Leave for a few minutes in tins before turning out onto a wire rack to continue cooling.

❹ For icing: Beat all ingredients together until smooth and creamy.

❺ Sandwich and top cake with icing. Decorate with grated chocolate.

VARIATIONS

Add 10 ml grated orange rind to dry ingredients and 5 ml grated orange rind to chocolate icing.

Add 3 ml ground cinnamon and 5 ml instant coffee to dry ingredients.

Add 5 ml peppermint essence to ingredients and 3 ml to chocolate icing.

Substitute boiling water with strong black coffee for a delicious flavour.

ORANGE FRUIT RING

125 g margarine
250 ml sugar (200 g)
2 eggs
500 ml Snowflake cake flour (280 g)
5 ml baking powder
250 ml fruit cake mix (150 g)
10 ml grated orange rind
5 ml bicarbonate of soda
250 ml sour milk

SYRUP
125 ml sugar (100 g)
125 ml orange juice
30 ml lemon juice
5 ml grated orange rind

❶ Cream margarine and sugar together. Add eggs and beat well until light and fluffy.

❷ Sift flour and baking powder and add to creamed mixture. Add cake mix and orange rind.

❸ Dissolve bicarbonate of soda in sour milk and add to mixture.

❹ Spoon into a greased 22 cm ring cake tin and bake in a preheated oven at 180 °C (350 °F) for 45–50 minutes.

❺ For syrup: Mix ingredients together and boil for 2 minutes.

❻ Remove cake from oven and spoon syrup over hot cake.

TIP

When grating rind from oranges or lemons, do not grate the pith as it will give a bitter taste.

Clockwise from top right: Orange Fruit Ring, Chocolate Oil Cake, Nutty Cherry Cake and Carrot and Banana Cake.

CARROT CAKE

4 eggs
375 ml castor sugar (315 g)
250 ml cooking oil
500 ml Snowflake cake flour (280 g)
10 ml baking powder
3 ml salt
5 ml ground cinnamon
3 ml ground ginger
3 ml ground cloves
2 ml bicarbonate of soda
750 ml finely grated carrot (375 g)
125 ml seedless raisins (75 g)
125 ml chopped pecan nuts, optional (50 g)

CREAM CHEESE ICING
100 g butter or margarine
125 g smooth cottage cheese
500 ml icing sugar (250 g)
10 ml lemon juice

❶ Whisk eggs and sugar together until light and fluffy.

❷ Add oil and beat well.

❸ Sift dry ingredients together and add to beaten mixture. Fold in carrot, raisins and nuts.

❹ Pour mixture into two lined and greased 20 cm cake tins.

❺ Bake in a preheated oven at 180 °C (350 °F) for 35–40 minutes. Leave in the tin for a few minutes after removing from oven, before turning onto a wire rack to continue cooling.

❻ For icing: Combine all ingredients and mix until smooth.

❼ Spread icing on cooled cake.

TIP

As the layers are large, they can be iced individually, resulting in two separate cakes.

LOW-FAT CHEESECAKE

1 x 20 cm sponge cake layer (page 57)
25 ml gelatine
100 ml water
4 eggs, separated
300 ml sugar
500 g smooth cottage cheese
5 ml vanilla essence
250 ml fresh cream

TOPPING
410 g can strawberries
(drained, syrup reserved)
25 ml cornflour

❶ Divide sponge cake horizontally into three layers. Place one in bottom of 20 cm loose-bottomed cake tin. Freeze remaining layers for later use.

❷ Sponge gelatine in the 100 ml water and dissolve over hot water.

❸ Beat egg yolks and 250 ml sugar together in top of double boiler. Beat until light and fluffy while bringing to the boil.

❹ Remove from heat; stir in gelatine.

❺ Add cottage cheese and essence, and fold in beaten egg whites.

❻ Beat cream with remaining sugar and add to egg mixture, beating lightly until smooth.

❼ Pour mixture over cake layer and leave to set in refrigerator.

❽Arrange fruit on top of cheesecake.

❾ For syrup: Boil syrup from fruit in a saucepan; dissolve cornflour in syrup. Bring to the boil and simmer while stirring constantly until thickened.

❿ Spoon syrup over fruit and leave to set in refrigerator.

TIPS

Sponging: Sprinkle powdered gelatine over cold water, leave for a few minutes to allow the gelatine to swell, then dissolve over boiling water.

Divide a cake layer by pulling strong gut or thread horizontally through it.

RED VELVET CAKE

125 g butter
250 ml sugar (200 g)
2 eggs
50 ml cocoa powder
30 ml red food colouring (1 bottle)
500 ml Snowflake cake flour (280 g)
2 ml salt
250 ml buttermilk
5 ml bicarbonate of soda
15 ml vinegar
5 ml vanilla essence

ICING
65 ml Snowflake cake flour (35 g)
250 ml milk
80 g butter
125 ml sugar (100 g)
5 ml vanilla essence
200 ml desiccated coconut (60 g)
25 g walnuts, chopped

❶ Beat butter and sugar together. Add eggs, one at a time, beating well until light and fluffy.

❷ Make a paste of cocoa and food colouring. Add to butter mixture and beat well.

❸ Sift flour and salt and add alternately with buttermilk to creamed mixture.

❹ Dissolve bicarbonate of soda in vinegar and add, with vanilla essence, to mixture.

❺ Spoon mixture into two greased 20 cm cake tins and bake in a preheated oven at 180 °C (350 °F) for 25–30 minutes.

❻ Leave in tin for a few minutes before turning out onto a wire rack to cool.

❼ For icing: Beat flour and milk together and bring to boil, stirring constantly until thickened.

❽ Remove from heat and stir in remaining ingredients.

❾ Ice cake when completely cold.

TIP

Instead of icing the cake, make an attractive pattern by dusting it with icing sugar sprinkled over a cooling rack or patterned doily.

FRIENDSHIP CAKE

500 ml Snowflake cake flour (280 g)
10 g instant dry yeast (1 sachet)
500 ml lukewarm water

Combine all ingredients and leave to stand, covered, for seven days, stirring once a day. Use 250 ml of this mixture to start your cake.

Day 1: Add 250 ml sugar, 250 ml cake flour, 250 ml milk. Leave to rise.

Days 2, 3 and 4: Stir well. Cover and leave to rise.

Day 5: Again add 250 ml sugar, 250 ml cake flour, 250 ml milk.

Days 6, 7, 8 and 9: Stir well. Cover and leave to rise.

Day 10: Stir. Give 250 ml of mixture and the recipe to each of three friends, keeping 250 ml. Make a delicious cake by adding to your mixture:

250 ml cooking oil
3 eggs, beaten
250 ml sugar (200 g)
500 ml Snowflake cake flour (280 g)
10 ml baking powder
5 ml bicarbonate of soda
10 ml vanilla essence
5 ml ground cinnamon
3 ml ground ginger
2 ml mixed spice
2 ml ground cloves
385 g can pie apples, chopped
250 ml fruit cake mix (150 g)
125 ml chopped walnuts, optional (50 g)
250 ml desiccated coconut, optional (80 g)
icing sugar for dusting

❶ Stir all ingredients together well.

❷ Spoon into a greased 22 cm ring tin or two greased 23 cm loaf tins and bake in a preheated oven at 160 °C (325 °F) for 45 minutes (ring tin) or 50–60 minutes (loaf tin).

❸ Dust with icing sugar and serve hot or cold with cream.

TIP

If mixture more than doubles in size during standing, just stir again.

Clockwise from top left: Red Velvet Cake, Friendship Cake and Low-Fat Cheesecake.

VENETIAN CAKE

65 g butter
65 ml sugar (50 g)
2 eggs
500 ml Snowflake cake flour (280 g)
2 ml salt
10 ml baking powder
10 ml vanilla essence

FILLING
625 ml milk
65 ml sugar (50 g)
2 egg yolks
15 ml Snowflake cake flour
20 ml custard powder
5 ml vanilla essence

❶ In a saucepan, melt butter, transfer to mixing bowl and beat in sugar. Add eggs, beating well after each addition.

❷ Sift dry ingredients together and add, with essence, to egg mixture.

❸ Mix to a stiff dough. Cover with plastic wrap and rest for about 1 hour.

❹ Divide dough into six equal portions. Roll out each portion to cover base of an inverted, greased, round cake tin. Trim, reserving excess dough.

❺ Bake each layer for 4–5 minutes in a preheated oven at 200 °C (400 °F) until light brown.

❻ For filling: Bring milk and sugar to the boil.

❼ Beat egg yolks, flour and custard powder together with a little extra milk to make a smooth paste.

❽ Pour a little of the boiled sugar mixture into egg yolk mixture and then pour this mixture back into the rest of heated mixture. Return to stove and cook until thick, boiling for approximately 5 minutes. Add essence.

❾ Use filling to sandwich the six biscuit layers together, spreading the remaining filling on top. Sprinkle with extra dough, baked and crushed.

VARIATION

As an alternative filling, use tinned caramel, slightly thinned, or any instant pudding such as vanilla or butterscotch.

BLACK FOREST GÂTEAU

CHOCOLATE CAKE
3 eggs
250 ml castor sugar (210 g)
50 ml water
50 ml milk
50 ml butter or margarine
50 ml cocoa powder
375 ml Snowflake cake flour (210 g)
10 ml baking powder
2 ml salt
5 ml vanilla essence

❶ For cake: Whisk eggs and sugar together until light and fluffy.

❷ Bring water, milk and butter to boil. Mix in cocoa powder.

❸ Sift flour, baking powder and salt together. Add to egg and sugar mixture gradually, beating continuously.

❹ Add boiled mixture and essence.

❺ Pour into two greased and lined 20 cm round cake tins and bake in a preheated oven at 180 °C (350 °F) for 25–30 minutes.

❻ Leave in tins for a few minutes before turning onto a wire rack to cool. Cut each layer horizontally into two.

FILLING AND TOPPING
10 ml sherry or kirsch liqueur
425 g can black cherries, without stones, in syrup
750 ml cream, whipped
200 g Albany chocolate, grated

❶ To assemble: Mix sherry with 125 ml cherry syrup.

❷ Place one layer of cake onto a serving platter. Sprinkle with some of the cherry syrup.

❸ Cover with a thin layer of cream.

❹ Halve three-quarters of the cherries. Place a third of the halved cherries on the layer of cream.

❺ Place a second layer of cake over this and repeat until final cake layer has been used. Press layers down gently.

❻ Cover sides of cake with cream and sprinkle chocolate around sides.

❼ Spread a layer of cream over top and pipe rosettes of cream around edge.

❽ Place a drained whole cherry on each rosette and sprinkle chocolate curls in the centre of the cake.

TIP

To coat the sides of cake: Place decoration such as chopped nuts, chocolate vermicelli or grated chocolate on a sheet of greaseproof paper. Holding the cake at top and bottom, roll in the decoration until the sides are evenly coated.

EGGLESS CAKE

500 ml Snowflake self-raising flour (280 g)
10 ml baking powder
3 ml bicarbonate of soda
125 g butter, melted
397 g can condensed milk
about 150 ml water
5 ml vanilla essence

❶ Sift flour, baking powder and bicarbonate of soda together.

❷ Cool butter slightly and add, with condensed milk, water and essence, to dry ingredients.

❸ Beat until smooth and spoon into two greased and lined 20 cm cake tins.

❹ Bake in a preheated oven at 180 °C (350 °F) for 20 minutes. Leave in tins for a few minutes before turning onto a wire rack to cool. Ice with Granadilla (page 66) or Lemon Icing (page 66).

TIP

This cake is suitable for cutting into shapes, and can be used as a base for fancy birthday cakes.

From top: Venetian Cake and Black Forest Gâteau.

CINNAMON CAKE

3 eggs, separated
250 ml sugar (200 g)
125 ml oil
125 ml water
250 ml Snowflake cake flour (140 g)
30 ml cornflour
15 ml baking powder
2 ml salt
30 ml ground cinnamon

SYRUP
30 g butter
50 ml smooth apricot or plum jam
cinnamon sugar

❶ Whisk egg yolks, sugar, oil and water together.

❷ Sift dry ingredients together and add to above mixture.

❸ Beat egg whites until stiff and fold into mixture.

❹ Pour into a greased ovenproof dish about 18 cm x 28 cm.

❺ Bake in a preheated oven at 190 °C (375 °F) for 20–30 minutes.

❻ For syrup: Melt butter and jam.

❼ Take cake out of oven and prick well. Pour hot syrup over hot cake.

❽ Sprinkle with cinnamon sugar and serve hot.

TIPS

To make cinnamon sugar, mix 100 ml sugar with 10 ml ground cinnamon.

Cinnamon is usually bought ready-ground for use in sweet and savoury dishes and in cakes.

SWISS ROLL

4 eggs, separated
165 ml castor sugar (140 g)
50 ml cold water
200 ml Snowflake self-raising flour (110 g)
2 ml salt
smooth jam, any flavour
icing sugar

❶ Whisk egg yolks; gradually add sugar, whisking all the time, until thick. Whisk in cold water.

❷ Beat egg whites until stiff but not dry, and add, with the sifted dry ingredients, to egg yolk mixture. Fold in gently with a metal spoon.

❸ Line a 23 cm x 32 cm Swiss roll tin with greaseproof paper. Grease well and turn mixture into tin. Bake in a preheated oven at 180 °C (350 °F) for 20 minutes.

❹ Turn out immediately onto a cloth well sprinkled with castor sugar. Peel off paper lining and trim edges of cake using a sharp knife. Roll up cake with cloth to make Swiss roll. Cover with a damp cloth and allow to cool slightly.

❺ Place jam in a double boiler over hot water until warm. Unroll cake and spread with jam. Roll up with the aid of a cloth and allow to cool. Dust lightly with icing sugar before serving.

VARIATIONS

Fill with strawberry or apricot jam and cream beaten with 65 ml grated or chopped chocolate.

CHOCOLATE SWISS ROLL

Add 25 ml cocoa powder and 3 ml instant coffee powder to the dry ingredients. Fill with beaten cream and sprinkle with a grated Peppermint Crisp or chopped chocolate. Roll up.

HAZELNUT SWISS ROLL

Add 125 ml chopped or ground toasted hazelnuts to the dry ingredients.

TIPS

The cake will roll best while still warm, so speed is essential for producing an unbroken and evenly rolled cake.

Make sure that the cake is completely cold before spreading with the filling.

GREEK SEMOLINA CAKE

350 g butter
250 ml sugar (200 g)
6 eggs, separated
10 ml grated orange rind
500 ml Snowflake cake flour (280 g)
250 ml semolina (160 g)
20 ml baking powder
2 ml salt
250 ml orange juice
80 ml almond flakes (50 g)

SYRUP
500 ml sugar (400 g)
500 ml water
30 ml brandy (optional)

❶ Beat butter and 125 ml of the sugar together. Add egg yolks and beat well after each addition until light and fluffy. Add orange rind.

❷ Beat egg whites until foamy. Add remaining sugar gradually, beating until egg whites are stiff, but not dry.

❸ Sift dry ingredients together and stir, with orange juice, into the creamed mixture. Fold in meringue.

❹ Turn into a greased 22 cm x 33 cm rectangular dish. Sprinkle with almonds.

❺ Bake in a preheated oven at 180 °C (350 °F) for 40–45 minutes. Allow to cool slightly.

❻ For syrup: Dissolve sugar in water and bring to the boil. Simmer for 5 minutes, add brandy, and pour over lukewarm cake.

❼ Cool and cut into squares.

VARIATION

Substitute brandy with Grand Marnier or Cointreau.

Clockwise from top: Hot Milk Sponge, Swiss Roll, Cinnamon Cake and Greek Semolina Cake.

HOT MILK SPONGE

4 eggs
300 ml castor sugar (250 g)
500 ml Snowflake cake flour (280 g)
15 ml baking powder
250 ml milk
100 g butter or margarine
5 ml vanilla essence

❶ Beat eggs and sugar together until thick and light yellow.

❷ Sift flour and baking powder together and fold into egg and sugar mixture.

❸ Heat milk and butter. Do not boil.

❹ Stir milk mixture and essence into batter. Spoon into two greased 20 cm cake tins.

❺ Bake in a preheated oven at 180 °C (350 °F) for 25–30 minutes.

TIPS

Use hot milk sponge for birthday cakes for the children, for baked Alaska or for trifle.

Make sure that the cake has cooled completely before you begin icing.

APPLE CAKE

2 eggs
250 ml sugar (200 g)
65 ml milk
30 g margarine, melted
250 ml Snowflake self-raising flour (140 g)
385 g can pie apples

SAUCE
250 ml sugar (200 g)
125 ml fresh cream
5 ml caramel essence

❶ Whisk eggs and sugar. Add milk and melted margarine.

❷ Add flour, mix until smooth, and pour batter into a greased dish about 18 cm x 28 cm, or a round 23 cm pie dish.

❸ Arrange apples on batter and bake in a preheated oven at 180 °C (350 °F) for 25–30 minutes, or until golden brown.

❹ For sauce: Combine sugar and cream, bring to the boil, and add essence. Pour over hot cake after removing from oven.

ORANGE BUTTER CAKE

250 g butter or margarine
300 ml castor sugar (250 g)
4 eggs
20 ml grated orange rind
5 ml vanilla essence
500 ml Snowflake self-raising flour (280 g)
2 ml salt
about 150 ml milk

❶ Cream butter and sugar together well. Add eggs, one at a time, and beat well after each addition until light and fluffy. Add orange rind and essence.

❷ Sift flour and salt together and add, together with milk, to egg mixture.

❸ Spoon into a greased and lined 20 cm x 24 cm rectangular tin.

❹ Bake in a preheated oven at 180 °C (350 °F) for 40–45 minutes.

❺ Leave in tin a while, then turn onto a wire rack to cool. Ice with Orange Icing (page 66). Cut into squares.

PETITS FOURS

GÉNOISE SPONGE
4 eggs
125 ml castor sugar (105 g)
250 ml Snowflake cake flour (140 g)
2 ml salt
60 g butter, melted and cooled

FILLING
125 ml smooth apricot jam (165 g)
20 ml water

TOPPING
250 g marzipan (almond paste)
icing sugar

GLACÉ ICING
750 ml icing sugar (400 g)
15 ml butter
about 30 ml boiling water
few drops vanilla, almond or orange essence or coffee powder
colouring of choice

❶ For sponge: Whisk eggs and sugar together until pale and thick.

❷ Sift flour and salt together; fold into mixture alternately with melted butter.

❸ Pour into a lined and greased 23 cm x 32 cm rectangular tin. Bake in a preheated oven at 180 °C (350 °F) for 15–20 minutes, until lightly browned and firm.

❹ Turn out onto wire rack, remove lining paper and cool completely. Divide cake into two horizontally.

❺ For filling: Heat apricot jam and water and brush half over one layer, covering with second layer. Press down well and brush the top of cake with remaining jam.

❻ For topping: Knead marzipan until smooth. Dust with icing sugar and roll out thinly into a rectangle. Cover sponge with marzipan. Place greaseproof paper over and leave for 24 hours. Remove paper and use cutters to cut into various shapes, such as triangles, ovals, squares and diamonds.

❼ For glacé icing: Mix all ingredients together to form a smooth and pouring consistency. Pour over petits fours to coat and leave to set. Decorate with chocolate, glacé cherries and angelica.

Makes 40

VARIATION

Substitute apricot jam with Chocolate Cream, and Glacé Icing with Chocolate Glacé Icing

CHOCOLATE CREAM

100 g butter
15 ml cocoa powder
3 ml coffee powder
20 ml boiling water
3 ml vanilla essence
250 ml icing sugar (130 g)
Beat all ingredients until light and thick.

CHOCOLATE GLACÉ ICING

Add 25 ml cocoa powder to icing sugar when making glacé icing.

CHOCOLATE BROWNIES

125 g dark cooking chocolate
125 g butter
15 ml golden syrup
3 eggs
500 ml sugar (400 g)
375 ml Snowflake cake flour (210 g)
1 ml salt
5 ml vanilla essence
125 ml chopped pecan nuts (50 g)

❶ Melt chocolate, butter and syrup together and mix until smooth.

❷ Beat eggs and sugar together until light and fluffy.

❸ Sift dry ingredients together and add, with melted chocolate mixture, to creamed egg mixture.

❹ Add essence and nuts.

❺ Pour mixture into a greased 20 cm x 24 cm rectangular tin and bake in a preheated oven at 160 °C (325 °F) for 40–45 minutes.

❻ Cool completely in tin, then cut into squares.

Makes 20

Clockwise from top: Petits Fours, Orange Butter Cake and Apple Cake.

LAMINGTONS

250 g butter or margarine
500 ml sugar (400 g)
4 eggs
125 ml milk
750 ml Snowflake cake flour (420 g)
10 ml baking powder
2 ml salt

CHOCOLATE SYRUP
750 ml sugar (600 g)
200 ml cocoa powder (80 g)
375 ml water
15 ml butter or margarine
desiccated coconut

❶ Beat butter and sugar together. Add eggs, and beat well after each addition until light and fluffy.

❷ Add milk and mix well.

❸ Sift flour, baking powder and salt together, and add to egg mixture.

❹ Spoon dough into a greased oven pan of about 25 cm x 30 cm or into two 23 cm square cake tins. Bake in a preheated oven at 180 °C (350 °F) for 50–60 minutes. Cut into squares and leave to cool.

❺ For syrup: Mix sugar, cocoa and water and bring to boil while stirring constantly. Add butter or margarine. While still warm, dip the cake squares in syrup, but do not soak. Roll squares in a thick layer of coconut spread on a large sheet of greaseproof paper.

❻ Place on a wire rack to set.

Makes 42

VARIATIONS

WHITE SYRUP

625 ml sugar (500 g)
250 ml water
3 egg whites

Bring sugar and water to boil, and boil for 5 minutes. Beat egg whites until stiff. Gradually pour syrup onto egg whites, and leave to cool.

COLOURED LAMINGTONS

For coloured lamingtons, colour coconut with food colourings.

TIPS

One-day-old cake is ideal for making lamingtons as it cuts more easily when a little stale. Alternatively, place in the deep-freeze for a while for easier cutting. Sponge can be frozen for 3–6 months.

Spear each piece of cake with a fork and dip into syrup. Hold over bowl for a moment to allow syrup to set slightly.

BANANA AND WALNUT BREAD

60 g butter
125 ml castor sugar (105 g)
1 egg, beaten
3 large bananas, mashed (250 ml)
500 ml Snowflake self-raising flour (280 g)
3 ml salt
75 ml milk
75 ml coarsely chopped walnuts, optional (30 g)
5 ml vanilla essence

❶ Beat butter and sugar together until the mixture is light and creamy.

❷ Add egg and mashed bananas, beating thoroughly.

❸ Sift flour and salt together and add alternately with milk to creamed mixture. Add walnuts and essence.

❹ Pour into a greased 23 cm loaf tin and bake in a preheated oven at 180 °C (350 °F) for 1 hour.

❺ Leave in tin for a few minutes before turning onto a wire rack to cool. Serve with butter.

TIP

To prevent the bowl from slipping while mixing, and to reduce noise, place a damp cloth underneath your mixing bowl.

CHOCOLATE PUMPKIN LOAF

125 g butter
10 ml grated orange rind
125 ml castor sugar (105 g)
1 egg
15 ml golden syrup
250 ml well-drained cold, mashed pumpkin (225 g)
300 ml Snowflake self-raising flour (165 g)
2 ml bicarbonate of soda
30 ml cocoa powder
15 ml custard powder
65 ml orange juice

ICING
250 ml icing sugar (130 g)
15 ml cocoa powder
5 ml butter
15 ml milk

❶ Beat butter, rind and sugar together. Add egg and syrup and beat well.

❷ Stir in pumpkin and dry ingredients alternately with orange juice.

❸ Pour mixture into a lined and greased 23 cm loaf tin and bake in a preheated oven at 180 °C (350 °F) for 1 hour. Leave loaf in the tin for a few minutes before turning onto a wire rack to cool.

❹ For icing: Sift icing sugar, add remaining ingredients, and beat until smooth. Spread icing over cooled loaf.

TIP

Cake can be stored in the refrigerator for a few days.

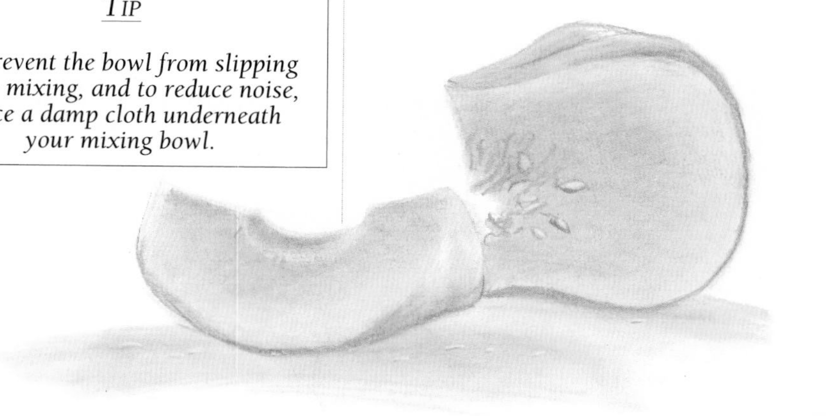

Clockwise from top: Lamingtons, Chocolate Pumpkin Loaf and Banana and Walnut Bread.

YOGHURT LOAF

125 g butter
15 ml grated orange rind
250 ml castor sugar (210 g)
3 eggs, separated
125 ml mixed peel (75 g)
65 ml orange juice
500 ml Snowflake self-raising flour (280 g)
250 ml low-fat plain yoghurt

ORANGE ICING
375 ml icing sugar (200 g)
30 g soft butter
5 ml grated orange rind
30 ml orange juice

❶ Beat butter, rind and sugar together in a bowl until light and creamy. Beat in egg yolks one at a time. Stir in mixed peel and orange juice.

❷ Sift flour and add to mixture alternately with yoghurt.

❸ Beat egg whites until soft peak stage and fold lightly into mixture.

❹ Pour mixture into a lined and greased 23 cm loaf tin and bake in a preheated oven at 150 °C (300 °F) for 1¼ hours. Leave in tin for a few minutes, then cool on a wire rack.

❺ For icing: Combine icing sugar, butter and rind. Stir in enough juice to mix icing to a spreading consistency. Ice cake.

TIP

It is best to remove the lining paper only once the cake has cooled.

GINGERBREAD

500 ml Snowflake cake flour (280 g)
5 ml baking powder
10 ml ground ginger
2 ml mixed spice
2 ml salt
3 ml bicarbonate of soda
125 ml brown sugar (100 g)
165 ml golden syrup
65 g margarine
2 eggs
200 ml milk
65 ml chopped preserved ginger

❶ Sift dry ingredients together, and add brown sugar.

❷ Melt syrup and margarine together, but do not boil.

❸ Whisk eggs and milk together.

❹ Gradually stir syrup mixture into egg mixture.

❺ Make a well in the centre of the dry ingredients and stir in liquid and preserved ginger. Beat well until smooth.

❻ Pour into a well-greased 23 cm loaf tin. Bake in a preheated oven at 160 °C (325 °F) for 1¼ hours.

VARIATION

MUFFINS

Add 125 ml sultanas to ingredients. Spoon into well-greased muffin tins and bake in a preheated oven at 180 °C (350 °F) for 20 minutes.

CHERRY LOAF

200 g soft butter or margarine
1 egg, beaten
5 ml vanilla essence
625 ml Snowflake cake flour (350 g)
10 ml baking powder
2 ml salt
160 ml halved red glacé cherries (100 g)
125 ml water
1 x 225 g tin condensed milk

❶ Cream butter, and add egg and essence. Sift dry ingredients together, and add cherries. Add, with remaining ingredients, to creamed mixture.

❷ Spoon into a lined and greased 23 cm loaf tin.

❸ Bake in a preheated oven at 190 °C (375 °F) for 50–60 minutes.

❹ Turn onto a wire rack to cool.

TIPS

This cake can be successfully made in a food processor.

Roll cherries in flour to prevent them from sinking to the bottom.

DATE LOAF

250 g pitted dates, chopped
5 ml bicarbonate of soda
250 ml boiling water
30 ml margarine
200 ml sugar (160 g)
1 egg
500 ml Snowflake cake flour (280 g)
5 ml baking powder
1 ml salt
5 ml vanilla essence

❶ Place dates in a bowl. Dissolve bicarbonate of soda in boiling water and pour over dates.

❷ Beat margarine and sugar together. Add egg, beating until light and fluffy.

❸ Sift dry ingredients and add alternately with dates and water to egg mixture. Add essence.

❹ Spoon mixture into a lined and greased 23 cm loaf tin and bake in a preheated oven at 160 °C (325 °F) for 50–55 minutes.

❺ Leave loaf in tin for a few minutes before turning out onto a wire rack to cool.

TIP

Dates can be bought whole, as plump and shiny table dates, to be eaten as they are, or pressed into slabs suitable for cooking.

Clockwise from top left: Cherry Loaf, Date Loaf, Nutty Almond Cake and Yoghurt Loaf.

NUTTY ALMOND CAKE

200 ml sugar (160 g)
125 ml cooking oil
125 ml milk
625 ml Snowflake self-raising flour (350 g)
1 ml salt
200 g smooth cottage cheese

TOPPING
150 g butter, melted
200 ml sugar (160 g)
50 ml desiccated coconut
170 ml almond flakes (100 g)
170 ml sprinkle nuts (100 g)

❶ Whisk sugar, oil and milk together.

❷ Sift flour and salt together and add to sugar mixture.

❸ Add cottage cheese and mix well.

❹ Spread on the base of a greased 22 cm x 33 cm rectangular dish or cake tin.

❺ For topping: Mix all ingredients together; spread over cake mixture.

❻ Bake in a preheated oven at 200 °C (400 °F) for 10 minutes and then reduce heat to 180 °C (350 °F) and bake for a further 20 minutes.

❼ Cool and cut into squares or slices.

VARIATION

Substitute nuts with coconut if preferred.

MADEIRA CAKE

125 g butter
250 ml castor sugar (210 g)
2 eggs
10 ml grated lemon rind
5 ml vanilla essence
500 ml Snowflake cake flour (280 g)
10 ml baking powder
250 ml milk

❶ Beat butter and sugar together well.

❷ Beat in eggs, lemon rind and essence until mixture is light and fluffy.

❸ Sift the flour and baking powder together and mix into the creamed mixture alternately with milk.

❹ Pour into a well-greased 23 cm loaf tin and bake in a preheated oven at 180 °C (350 °F) for 1 hour.

VARIATION

CARAWAY SEED CAKE

Add 10 ml caraway seeds to creamed mixture.

TIP

To soften butter in the microwave: Place in a small microwave bowl and cover with paper towel. Cook on high or 100% power until soft but not melted. 125 g butter takes about 45 seconds to soften.

EASY FRUIT LOAF

250 ml brown sugar (200 g)
250 ml milk
250 g butter or margarine
400 ml fruit cake mix (250 g)
100 ml chopped glacé cherries (60 g)
1 egg, beaten
625 ml Snowflake cake flour (350 g)
5 ml baking powder
3 ml bicarbonate of soda
5 ml mixed spice

❶ Place sugar, milk, butter, cake mix and cherries in a saucepan. Bring to boil, then simmer for 2–3 minutes. Allow to cool.

❷ Add beaten egg to mixture. Sift dry ingredients together, add to mixture, and mix well.

❸ Pour into a greased and well-lined 23 cm loaf tin.

❹ Bake in a preheated oven at 160 °C (325 °F) for 1¼ hours. Leave for a few minutes in tin before turning onto a wire rack to cool.

TIP

Test whether the cake is cooked by inserting a skewer into the centre. If it is baked, the skewer will come out clean.

VARIATIONS

Pour this syrup over hot loaf:
125 ml fresh orange juice
10 ml fresh lemon juice
3 ml grated orange rind
125 ml sugar (100 g)
Boil ingredients together for 5 minutes, then leave to cool slightly before pouring over cake.

Add 125 ml chopped pecan nuts or walnuts to mixture.

BABY MARROW LOAF

250 ml cooking oil
250 ml sugar (200 g)
3 eggs
500 ml Snowflake cake flour (280 g)
250 ml Snowflake Nutty Wheat (150 g)
5 ml baking powder
2 ml bicarbonate of soda
2 ml salt
1 ml nutmeg
15 ml ground cinnamon
500 ml finely grated baby marrow (250 g)
125 ml seedless raisins (75 g)
5 ml vanilla essence

❶ Whisk oil and sugar together. Add eggs, beating well after each addition.

❷ Sift dry ingredients together, add bran left behind in sieve, and add, alternately with baby marrow, to creamed mixture.

❸ Stir in raisins and essence and spoon into a lined 23 cm loaf tin. Bake in a preheated oven at 160 °C (325 °F) for 50–60 minutes.

TIPS

Large baby marrows are delicious hollowed out and stuffed with a savoury filling such as onion, cheese, bacon and parsley, and then grilled or baked.

It is not necessary to peel baby marrows before cooking.

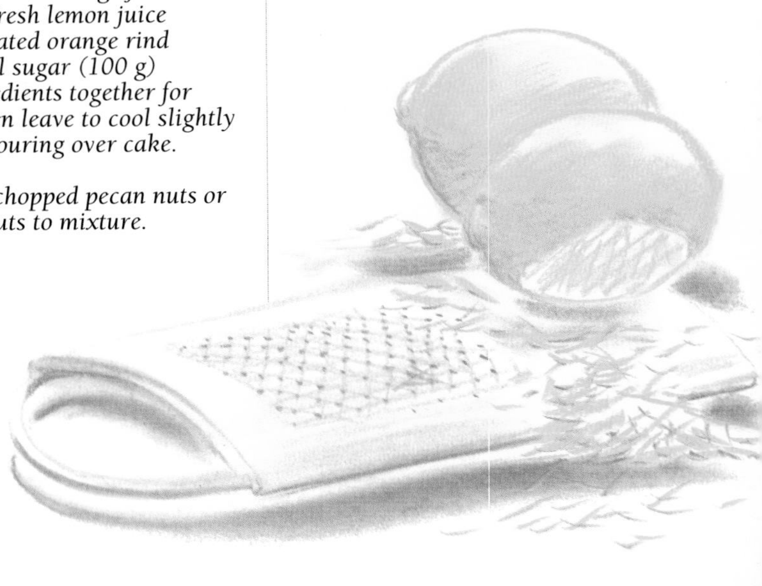

Clockwise from top: Baby Marrow Loaf, Easy Fruit Loaf and Madeira Cake.

CAKE ICING

Icing is more than just a decoration on cakes. It prevents drying out and adds flavour to bland cakes or biscuits.

Colour and flavour the icing according to your personal taste.

Hints for icing cakes

- Allow cake to cool completely before icing. If cake is still slightly warm, icing will melt and run off surface.
- Brush all loose crumbs off surface of cake before icing.
- The icing surface should be flat. Turn cake over and use base or, alternatively, trim top of cake to level it.
- Delicate cakes should be iced with soft icing to prevent the cake from crumbling.
- When coating a cake with soft icing, do so on a wire rack. Spread icing while soft, using a palette knife.
- If a filling and an icing are used, place filling between layers before icing the cake or biscuit.
- When icing a cake with butter icing, cover the sides of the cake before icing the top.
- If the sides of the cake are to be covered with nuts, praline or chocolate vermicelli, first sandwich the layers together, then cover the sides with icing. Turn the cake onto its side, and gently roll the edges in the coating of your choice.
- Do not overmix the icing as this will result in a runny mixture.

BASIC ICING

100 g soft butter
500 ml icing sugar (250 g)
10 ml vanilla essence
about 25 ml milk

❶ Cream butter, icing sugar and essence. Add enough milk to make mixture light and creamy, and of a spreadable consistency.

❷ Sandwich the layers together with icing, then ice the top of the cake.

CHOCOLATE BUTTER ICING

100 g soft butter
500 ml icing sugar (250 g)
30 ml cocoa powder
30 ml hot water
5 ml vanilla essence
about 25 ml milk

❶ Cream butter and icing sugar, beating well until smooth. Dissolve cocoa powder in hot water and add to icing.

❷ Add essence and enough milk to make mixture light and creamy, and of a spreadable consistency.

❸ Sandwich layers together with icing and ice the top of the cake.

MOCHA ICING

100 g soft butter
500 ml icing sugar (250 g)
30 ml cocoa powder
10 ml strong coffee powder
30 ml hot water
about 25 ml milk

❶ Cream butter and icing sugar. Dissolve cocoa powder and coffee powder in hot water and add to icing.

❷ Add enough milk to make mixture light and creamy, and of a spreadable consistency.

❸ Sandwich layers together with icing, then ice the top of the cake.

ORANGE ICING

60 g soft butter
500 ml icing sugar (250 g)
5 ml grated orange rind
50 ml orange juice

❶ Cream butter, icing sugar and rind together. Add enough juice to make mixture light and creamy, and of a spreadable consistency.

❷ Sandwich layers together with icing, then ice the top of the cake.

LEMON ICING

30 ml soft butter
375 ml icing sugar (200 g)
5 ml grated lemon rind
15 ml lemon juice

❶ Cream butter, icing sugar and rind together. Add enough juice to make mixture light and creamy, and of a spreadable consistency.

❷ Sandwich layers together with icing, then ice the top of the cake.

GRANADILLA ICING

25 ml soft butter
625 ml icing sugar (325 g)
115 g can granadilla pulp

❶ Cream butter, icing sugar and granadilla pulp until light and creamy, and of a spreadable consistency.

❷ Sandwich layers together with icing, then ice the top of the cake.

CARAMEL ICING

60 g soft butter
50 ml brown sugar (40 g)
375 ml icing sugar (200 g)
5 ml caramel essence
about 25 ml milk

❶ Cream butter and sugar together. Add icing sugar, essence and enough milk to make icing light and creamy.

❷ Sandwich layers together with icing, then ice the top of the cake.

Clockwise from top left: Chocolate Butter Icing, Lemon Icing, Granadilla Icing, Royal Icing, Orange Icing, Glacé Icing and Mocha Icing.

CREAM CHEESE ICING

100 g soft butter
500 ml icing sugar (250 g)
125 g smooth cottage cheese
5 ml vanilla essence

❶ Cream butter, icing sugar, cottage cheese and essence together until mixture is light and creamy, and has a spreadable consistency.

❷ Sandwich layers together with icing, then ice top of cake.

GLACÉ ICING

Use this icing while still warm. Glaze cake with apricot jam before icing so that no crumbs mix with the icing.

250 ml icing sugar (130 g)
about 30 ml boiling water
2 ml vanilla essence or lemon juice
few drops of food colouring

❶ Sift icing sugar and add enough water to make a smooth consistency.

❷ Add essence and colouring. Dip a skewer into the bottle and add to icing to avoid using too much colouring.

ROYAL ICING

This quick-and-easy fruit cake icing is traditionally used on top of a layer of marzipan and will protect the cake for months.

1 egg white
750 ml icing sugar (400 g)
5 ml lemon juice

❶ Beat egg white until foamy. Gradually beat in icing sugar, beating well after each addition.

❷ When mixture reaches soft peak stage, beat in lemon juice. Continue to add icing sugar and beat until stiff.

Muffins

MUFFINS ARE QUICK AND EASY TO MAKE USING SWEET OR SAVOURY INGREDIENTS AND CAN BE SERVED ON ANY DAY OF THE YEAR! ADD LOTS OF BRAN TO MAKE THEM NUTRITIOUS.
THE MUFFINS WE KNOW ARE USUALLY REFERRED TO AS AMERICAN MUFFINS TO DISTINGUISH THEM FROM ENGLISH MUFFINS, WHICH ARE ROUND YEAST CAKES SIMILAR TO CRUMPETS.

GUIDELINES FOR MAKING MUFFINS

- Handle batter lightly. Mix liquids into the dry ingredients, stirring just enough to moisten. The batter should still look lumpy.

- Overmixing the batter will destroy the light texture of the muffins and can result in tough, coarse muffins that contain tunnels.

- Fill the muffin tins two-thirds full, spooning in the batter in one scoop. If muffin tins are not available, spoon batter into paper cookie cases placed on a baking tray.

- To test whether they are done, press down gently on top of muffin. If it springs back, the muffins are ready.

- Muffins are best when freshly baked. They are delicious served warm and buttered.

Freezing muffins

Muffins can be successfully frozen for up to 3 months. Cool slightly, then while still warm, freeze in foil or an airtight container to preserve moisture. Reheat frozen in foil in an oven at 200 °C (400 °F) for 12–15 minutes. Alternatively, place 1 frozen muffin in paper towel in microwave on high or 100% power for 30–45 seconds.

30-DAY HEALTH MUFFINS

The mixture for these delicious, healthy muffins can be stored in an airtight container in the refrigerator for up to 30 days, and used as needed.

2 eggs
125 ml cooking oil
375 ml soft brown sugar (300 g)
500 ml milk
250 ml Snowflake Nutty Wheat (150 g)
375 ml Snowflake cake flour (210 g)
500 ml Snowflake digestive bran (60 g)
OR 250 ml Snowflake Nutty Wheat (150 g)
5 ml salt
5 ml vanilla essence
10 ml bicarbonate of soda
250 ml fruit cake mix (150 g)
150 g pitted dates, chopped

❶ Whisk eggs, oil and sugar together.

❷ Add remaining ingredients and mix until combined.

❸ Pour the mixture into an airtight container and allow to stand in the refrigerator overnight.

❹ Spoon into well-greased muffin tins, filling each two-thirds full. Bake in a preheated oven at 180 °C (350 °F) for 20–25 minutes.

❺ Serve hot with butter.

Makes 48

VARIATIONS

Add 250 ml chopped walnuts or pecan nuts to the mixture.

Substitute fruit cake mix and dates with 500 ml sultanas or raisins.

15 ml grated orange rind may also be added to ingredients.

BLUEBERRY MUFFINS

125 ml Snowflake Nutty Wheat (75 g)
250 ml Snowflake cake flour (140 g)
15 ml baking powder
200 ml castor sugar (170 g)
3 ml salt
1 egg
125 ml milk
100 ml oil
425 g can blueberries, well drained

❶ Sift dry ingredients together and add bran left behind in sieve.

❷ Whisk egg, milk and oil together and mix into dry ingredients. Mix until flour is moistened; batter should still be lumpy. Add blueberries, being careful not to overmix.

❸ Spoon into greased muffin tins, filling each two-thirds full. Bake in a preheated oven at 200 °C (400 °F) for 15–20 minutes, until golden brown.

❹ Serve hot with butter.

Makes 12

VARIATION

YOUNGBERRY MUFFINS

Substitute blueberries with a can of youngberries.

TIP

These muffins are not suitable for freezing.

From top: Blueberry Muffins and 30-day Health Muffins.

APPLE AND RAISIN MUFFINS

125 g margarine
125 ml sugar (100 g)
2 eggs
385 g can pie apples, chopped
125 ml raisins (75 g)
250 ml milk
2 ml vanilla essence
500 ml Snowflake cake flour (280 g)
OR
250 ml Snowflake Nutty Wheat (150 g) and 250 ml Snowflake cake flour (140 g)
20 ml baking powder
2 ml salt
cinnamon sugar

❶ Beat margarine and sugar together. Add eggs and beat until mixture is light and fluffy.

❷ Stir in apples, raisins, milk and essence until thoroughly mixed. Add to sifted dry ingredients and mix until flour is moistened; batter should still be lumpy.

❸ Spoon into greased muffin tins, filling each about two-thirds full and sprinkle with cinnamon sugar. Bake in a preheated oven at 200 °C (400 °F) for 20–25 minutes.

❹ Serve hot with butter.

Makes 18

VARIATIONS

PINEAPPLE MUFFINS

Substitute apples and raisins with 425 g can crushed pineapple, with syrup.

CARROT MUFFINS

Substitute apples with 375 ml grated carrot, and add 2 ml allspice and 5 ml ground cinnamon to dry ingredients.

TIP

To soften hardened sugar, place a lemon in the sugar jar; after a few hours the sugar will have softened.

NUTTY WHEAT BANANA AND DATE MUFFINS

250 ml Snowflake Nutty Wheat (150 g)
5 ml baking powder
3 ml ground cinnamon
250 ml wheatgerm (80 g)
1 egg
80 ml cooking oil
125 ml brown sugar (100 g)
5 ml bicarbonate of soda
50 ml milk
2 bananas, mashed (about 180 ml)
60 g pitted dates, chopped

❶ Sift Nutty Wheat, baking powder and ground cinnamon together. Add bran left in sieve and wheatgerm.

❷ Whisk egg, oil and sugar together, and mix into dry ingredients.

❸ Dissolve bicarbonate of soda in milk and stir, with bananas and dates, into dry ingredients. Mix until flour is moistened; batter should still be lumpy. Do not overmix.

❹ Spoon mixture into greased muffin tins, filling each two-thirds full.

❺ Bake in a preheated oven at 200 °C (400 °F) for 20 minutes. Leave in tin a few minutes before turning onto a wire rack to cool.

❻ Serve hot with butter.

Makes 12

NUTTY WHEAT MARMALADE MUFFINS

375 ml Snowflake Nutty Wheat (225 g)
250 ml Snowflake cake flour (140 g)
20 ml baking powder
3 ml salt
75 ml oil
250 ml milk
2 eggs
125 ml soft brown sugar (100 g)
125 ml fruit cake mix (75 g)
75 ml orange marmalade (100 g)

❶ Sift dry ingredients together. Add bran left behind in sieve.

❷ Whisk oil, milk, eggs and sugar together. Add fruit cake mix and marmalade.

❸ Add liquid ingredients to dry ingredients; mix until flour is moistened. Batter should still be lumpy.

❹ Spoon mixture into muffin tins until half-full. Spoon one teaspoonful of marmalade on top and then cover with more mixture until muffin tins are two-thirds full.

❺ Bake in a preheated oven at 180 °C (350 °F) for 15–20 minutes.

Makes 12

VARIATIONS

Any jam can be used instead of marmalade.

As an alternative, the marmalade or jam can be mixed into the batter.

Clockwise from top left: Nutty Wheat Marmalade Muffins, Apple and Raisin Muffins and Nutty Wheat Banana and Date Muffins.

DATE AND WALNUT MUFFINS

500 ml Snowflake cake flour (280 g)
10 ml baking powder
3 ml salt
80 ml brown sugar (65 g)
65 g margarine
120 g pitted dates, chopped
125 ml chopped walnuts OR pecan nuts (50 g)
125 ml milk
1 egg

❶ Sift flour, baking powder and salt. Add sugar. Rub in margarine; add dates and nuts.

❷ Whisk milk and egg, and mix into dry ingredients. Mix until flour is moistened; batter should still be lumpy.

❸ Spoon mixture into greased muffin tins, filling each two-thirds full.

❹ Bake in a preheated oven at 190 °C (375 °F) for 20 minutes.

❺ Serve hot with butter.

Makes 12

TIP

Chop dates using a knife that has been dipped in flour

LEMON MUFFINS

125 g margarine
125 ml castor sugar (105 g)
2 eggs
450 ml Snowflake cake flour (250 g)
5 ml baking powder
3 ml bicarbonate of soda
1 ml salt
10 ml grated lemon rind
100 ml lemon juice

❶ Beat margarine and sugar together. Add eggs and beat until light and fluffy.

❷ Sift dry ingredients and add, with rind and juice, to creamed mixture until flour is moistened; batter should still be lumpy. Do not overmix.

❸ Spoon mixture into greased muffin tins, filling each two-thirds full. Bake in a preheated oven at 200 °C (400 °F) for 20 minutes.

❹ Serve hot with butter.

Makes 12

TIP

A medium-sized lemon yields about 40 ml juice.To extract maximum juice, warm a whole lemon in a preheated moderate oven for 2 minutes.

SPINACH MUFFINS

375 ml Snowflake cake flour (210 g)
10 ml baking powder
3 ml salt
1 ml cayenne pepper
250 ml cooked chopped spinach (200 g)
125 g rindless streaky bacon, chopped
250 ml grated Cheddar cheese (100g)
100 ml milk
100 ml cooking oil
1 egg

❶ Sift dry ingredients together. Add spinach, raw bacon and grated cheese and mix slightly.

❷ Beat milk, oil and egg together, and stir into dry ingredients. Mix until flour is moistened; batter should still be lumpy. Spoon into greased muffin tins, filling each two-thirds full.

❸ Bake in a preheated oven at 190 °C (375 °F) for 15–20 minutes.

❹ Serve hot with butter.

Makes 12

TIPS

Rinse spinach several times in cold water. Cook in a saucepan without any water. The water left clinging to the leaves is sufficient for cooking. Cover tightly and cook until just wilted. Drain, refresh under cold running water, then squeeze well to remove as much moisture as possible.

Substitute fresh spinach with frozen, but drain off excess water.

CHEESE AND CHIVE MUFFINS

1 egg
200 ml milk
250 ml Snowflake cake flour (140 g)
10 ml baking powder
2 ml dry mustard
2 ml cayenne pepper
375 ml grated Cheddar cheese (150 g)
50 ml chopped chives

❶ In a measuring jug, beat egg lightly with a fork, then fill jug with milk to 250 ml measure.

❷ Sift dry ingredients together, add cheese and chives, and mix in liquid until flour is moistened; batter should still be lumpy.

❸ Spoon into greased muffin tins, filling each two-thirds full. Bake in a preheated oven at 200 °C (400 °F) for 15 minutes, until golden brown.

❹ Serve hot with butter.

Makes 8

VARIATIONS

Add 50 ml chopped parsley and/or onion to mixture.

Add 75 ml chopped bacon, ham or viennas to mixture.

TIP

Cayenne pepper is a hot spice ground from red peppers and should be used sparingly. It can be used in curries, soups, sauces and dressings.

Clockwise from top left: Cheese and Chive Muffins, Spinach Muffins, Lemon Muffins and Date and Walnut Muffins.

7

BREADS

AS MORE AND MORE PEOPLE ARE ADOPTING A HEALTHY WAY OF LIVING, THERE IS AN INCREASING DEMAND FOR BREAD RECIPES USING WHOLEWHEAT FLOUR AND BRAN. NATURALLY, QUICK-AND-EASY RECIPES ARE ALWAYS POPULAR, TOO. THIS CHAPTER PROVIDES A SELECTION OF RECIPES THAT SATISFY BOTH REQUIREMENTS, AND ALSO INCLUDES A FEW FOR WHITE BREAD AND SOME INTERESTING VARIATIONS.

To use yeast successfully it is necessary to know how to use it, and the differences between the various types of yeast.

Instant dry yeast has been used in the recipes in this book because it is easy to use and is the only kind of yeast that is added directly to the dry ingredients. It is also convenient as it reduces rising time, and it's not necessary to dissolve it beforehand.

Instant dry yeast can be purchased in 10 g (15 ml) sachets. Once the sachet has been opened, the yeast will deteriorate and should therefore be used immediately. Sealed sachets of dry yeast can be stored in a cool, dry place for up to 18 months.

Active dry yeast and fresh cube yeast are also available – 10 g instant dry yeast is equivalent to one 25 g cube fresh yeast.

Kneading

This is the most important process in bread making. A good kneading technique is essential as this develops the protein, which is known as gluten, in the flour. As a result of kneading and stretching, the dough becomes elastic, which enables it to rise well and ensures that the product holds its shape.

Before beginning, lightly flour your hands and work surface. Use the palm of your hand to fold the dough repeatedly, working from the outside to the inside. If the dough becomes sticky, sprinkle it with a little flour, but avoid adding too much.

The amount of flour specified in a recipe is only a guide and may vary according to the humidity and the moisture content of the flour used.

Knead for up to 10 minutes, until the dough is smooth and elastic without being sticky. This can also be done successfully using the dough hook of an electric mixer.

Rising

Place the dough in a greased container and cover with plastic wrap or a damp cloth – this helps to retain moisture and prevents a thick skin from forming on the dough. Rising time will depend on temperature; the dough should double in size during rising. The dough will rise best in a warm, humid, draught-free place. To test whether dough has risen properly, press a finger into it. If the dough has risen sufficiently, the impression made by your finger should remain.

Knocking down

After it has risen, turn dough onto a floured surface and knead until it returns to its original volume. This will distribute the air bubbles that have developed throughout the dough during rising, and ensures an even texture. Knock down by pressing your knuckles repeatedly into the risen dough. Then shape the dough as desired. If making bread, fill half to two-thirds of pan with dough, placing the fold underneath. Brush bread or rolls with water and leave in a warm place to rise (or prove) once more, covering with plastic wrap or a damp towel as done for the first rising; leave to double in size once more.

Glazing

Glazing involves brushing the dough before baking with a glaze such as beaten egg or milk and protects the crust and improves the appearance of the bread. After glazing, sprinkle with seeds, nuts, crushed wheat or rolled oats. One can further improve the appearance of the bread by making shallow cuts across the top of the dough with a sharp knife or a pair of scissors, diagonally or in any other pattern.

Baking

Bread is usually baked at about 200 °C (400 °F). The high temperature destroys the yeast and stops its action.

Once cooked, the crust should have a good, rich colour. To test whether the loaf is baked, tap its base with your knuckles. If it sounds hollow, it is done. Cool on a wire rack.

Freezing

When completely cooled, wrap bread in plastic wrap and freeze for up to 3 months. Thaw at room temperature for 4–6 hours, or defrost in a microwave oven. Wrap in a damp paper towel and defrost on medium-low or 30 % power for 4 minutes, depending on size.

QUICK HEALTH BREAD

4 x 250 ml Snowflake Nutty Wheat (600 g)
5 ml salt
10 g instant dry yeast (1 sachet)
15 ml sesame seeds
15 ml poppy seeds
30 ml sunflower seeds
500 ml lukewarm water
30 ml cooking oil
30 ml honey or syrup
seeds or oats for topping

❶ Sift flour and salt together. Add bran left in sieve, yeast and seeds.

❷ Combine water, oil and honey and add to dry ingredients. Mix well.

❸ Spoon into a well-greased 23 cm loaf tin; sprinkle with seeds. Cover lightly with a damp towel and leave to rise in a warm place for 20–30 minutes. Bake in a preheated oven at 200 °C (400 °F) for 40–45 minutes.

Makes 1 loaf

VARIATION

Bake loaves in tins of different sizes.

Quick Health Bread baked in tins of various shapes and sizes.

WHOLEWHEAT BREAD

500 ml Snowflake Nutty Wheat (300 g)
500 ml Snowflake cake flour (280 g)
5 ml bicarbonate of soda
5 ml baking powder
5 ml salt
15 ml brown sugar
500 ml low-fat plain yoghurt
15 ml cooking oil
15 ml milk
crushed wheat or sesame seeds for topping

❶ Sift dry ingredients together and add bran left in sieve. Add sugar.

❷ Add yoghurt and oil. Add milk to empty yoghurt container, shake and add to mixture. Mix thoroughly.

❸ Spoon into a greased 23 cm loaf tin and sprinkle with crushed wheat or sesame seeds.

❹ Bake in a preheated oven at 180 °C (350 °F) for 45 minutes. Switch off the oven and leave bread inside for a further 15 minutes.

Makes 1 loaf

SEED LOAF

250 ml Snowflake white bread flour (140 g)
4 x 250 ml Snowflake Nutty Wheat (600 g)
10 ml salt
250 ml crushed wheat (200 g)
10 g instant dry yeast (1 sachet)
50 ml brown sugar (40 g)
50 ml sesame seeds
50 ml poppy seeds
50 ml linseeds
10 ml caraway seeds
100 ml sprinkle nuts, optional (60 g)
50 ml cooking oil
4 x 250 ml lukewarm water
extra seeds for topping

❶ Sift flour, Nutty Wheat and salt together. Add bran left behind in sieve and crushed wheat.

❷ Add yeast, sugar, seeds and nuts.

❸ Mix oil and lukewarm water together, then add to dry ingredients, mixing well.

❹ Spoon into two well-greased 23 cm loaf tins and sprinkle with seeds. Cover lightly with a damp towel and leave to rise in a warm place for 20–30 minutes. Bake in a preheated oven at 200 °C (400 °F) for 1 hour.

Makes 2 loaves

> TIP
>
> *If the water used for activating yeast is too hot, the yeast is killed; too cold, and it is not activated. Achieve the right temperature by mixing one-third boiling with two-thirds cold water.*

ONION AND CHEESE BREAD

875 ml Snowflake self-raising flour (500 g)
1 packet thick white onion OR brown onion soup powder
500 ml buttermilk
125 ml grated Cheddar cheese (50 g)
about 15 ml milk
pinch of cayenne pepper

❶ Mix flour, soup powder, buttermilk and half of the cheese together. Add milk to empty buttermilk container, shake, and add to mixture.

❷ Spoon into a lined and greased 23 cm loaf tin and sprinkle remaining cheese and cayenne pepper on top.

❸ Bake in a preheated oven at 180 °C (350 °F) for 1 hour. Serve with butter.

Makes 1 loaf

VARIATION

SAVOURY BREAD

Add 125 g ham or raw rindless bacon, chopped, to the ingredients.

> TIP
>
> *Buttermilk, made by adding a bacterial culture to low-fat or skimmed milk, is more suitable for baking than sour milk.*

CHEESE AND HERB TWIST

750 ml Snowflake brown bread meal (420 g)
7 ml salt
10 g instant dry yeast (1 sachet)
50 ml cooking oil
about 350 ml lukewarm water
500 ml grated Cheddar cheese (200 g) OR mozzarella cheese (250 g)
50 ml chopped fresh herbs OR 15 ml mixed dried herbs
10 ml crushed fresh garlic, optional

❶ Sift bread meal and salt together, adding bran left behind in sieve. Add dry yeast and mix.

❷ Add oil and lukewarm water and mix to a soft dough.

❸ Turn onto a lightly floured surface and knead dough for 10 minutes, until smooth and elastic. Place dough in an oiled bowl, cover, and allow to rest for 20 minutes.

❹ Knock down the dough and roll out into a rectangle of 30 cm x 35 cm.

❺ Sprinkle cheese, herbs and garlic over. Roll up from short side.

❻ Hold ends of roll and twist in opposite directions. Place on a greased baking tray.

❼ Slash six times across the top and allow to rise for 30–40 minutes.

❽ Bake in a preheated oven at 200 °C (400 °F) for 40 minutes. Serve hot.

Makes 1 loaf

Clockwise from top left: Onion and Cheese Bread, Seed Loaf, Wholewheat Bread and Cheese and Herb Twist.

BEER AND CHEESE BREAD

875 ml Snowflake self-raising flour (500 g)
5 ml salt
340 ml beer (1 dumpie)
125 ml grated Cheddar cheese (50 g)
about 30 ml water

❶ Place all ingredients in a mixing bowl, reserving half of cheese for topping, and mix together well. Add water if necessary.

❷ Spoon into a lined and greased 23 cm loaf tin and sprinkle remaining cheese on top.

❸ Bake in a preheated oven at 180 °C (350 °F) for 1 hour. Serve hot, with butter.

Makes 1 loaf

VARIATION

Substitute cheese with 125 ml grated biltong, and add 30 ml chopped fresh herbs or 10 ml dried herbs.

WHITE BREAD

7 x 250 ml Snowflake white bread flour (1 kg)
10 ml salt
10 ml sugar
10 g instant dry yeast (1 sachet)
20 ml margarine
about 650 ml lukewarm water

❶ Sift flour, salt and sugar together. Add dry yeast and mix.

❷ Rub margarine into dry ingredients and gradually add lukewarm water to mix to a soft dough. Add more water if needed.

❸ Turn out onto a lightly floured surface and knead dough for about 10 minutes, until smooth and elastic. Place dough in an oiled bowl, cover, and allow to rest for 20 minutes.

❹ Knock down the dough and divide into two. Place each portion in a greased 23 cm loaf tin, cover with oiled plastic wrap, and leave to rise in a warm place for 30–40 minutes, until double in size.

❺ Brush top with water and bake in a preheated oven at 200 °C (400 °F) for 35 minutes.

Makes 2 loaves

TIP

To test whether bread is done, turn it upside down after baking and tap the bottom with your knuckles. If it sounds hollow, it is baked.

VARIATIONS

BROWN BREAD

Follow recipe for white bread, but substitute white bread flour with brown bread meal.

POT BREAD

Follow recipe for white bread, but increase the amount of margarine to 65 g. After the first rising, knock down, form the dough into one large round loaf, and place in a greased, heavy-based pot. Cover and allow to rise until double in volume. Brush with milk or beaten egg. Bake for 45–50 minutes.

VETKOEK

Follow recipe for white bread, but increase the amount of margarine to 65 g. After first rising, knock down and divide dough into 36 pieces. Cover and allow to rise until double in volume. Fry in hot oil.

ROOSTERKOEK

Follow recipe for Vetkoek, but cook over the braai on a grid or in an unoiled griddle pan on the stove.

ASKOEK

Follow recipe for Vetkoek, but when dividing dough, make bigger balls. Place balls in warm ashes, but not directly on the coals. Leave for 30 minutes, then remove.

BREAD STICKS (GRISSINI)

Follow recipe for white bread, but increase the amount of margarine to 65 g. After the first rising, knock down and divide dough into sticks about 12 cm long. Place on a greased baking tray. Brush with milk or beaten egg; sprinkle with coarse salt, sesame seeds or poppy seeds. Cover and leave to rise until double in volume. Bake at 220 °C (425 °F) for 12–15 minutes, until golden brown and crisp. Store in an airtight container.

STOKBROOD

Follow recipe for white bread. After the first rising, knock down and divide dough into 12 even portions. Roll into long sausages and roll around 12 skewers. Braai stokbrood over cooled coals until done. Remove skewers and fill holes with butter and syrup.

FOCCACIA

This is a savoury Italian flat bread, which can be flavoured with fresh herbs and garlic if desired.

1 quantity Pizza Dough (page 14)
50 ml olive oil or garlic butter
coarse salt
fresh rosemary or sage, chopped

❶ Follow recipe for pizza dough.

❷ After the first rising, knock down and divide into two rounds. Flatten on greased baking tray or two 25 cm pizza plates.

❸ Brush with olive oil or garlic butter, and sprinkle with salt and rosemary or sage. Cover with plastic wrap and leave to rise in a warm place until double in size – for 15–20 minutes.

❹ Bake in a preheated oven at 200 °C (400 °F) for 20 minutes, or until golden brown.

❺ Serve hot, cut into wedges.

Makes 2 loaves

VARIATION

For garlic lovers, crush 4 cloves garlic and sprinkle over dough.

BRAN AND RAISIN LOAF

625 ml Snowflake self-raising flour (350 g)
2 ml salt
250 ml Snowflake digestive bran (30 g)
250 ml brown sugar (200 g)
125 ml seedless raisins (75 g)
375 ml milk

❶ Sift flour and salt together. Mix in all other ingredients.

❷ Pour mixture into a greased and lined 23 cm loaf tin and bake in a preheated oven at 190 °C (375 °F) for 50–55 minutes. Serve hot with butter.

Makes 1 loaf

Clockwise from top left: Bran and Raisin Loaf, White Bread, Bread Sticks, Vetkoek, Foccacia, Roosterkoek, Stokbrood and Pot Bread.

SOFT ROLLS

4 x 250 ml Snowflake cake flour (560 g)
5 ml salt
20 ml sugar
20 ml milk powder
10 g instant dry yeast (1 sachet)
30 ml margarine
about 250 ml lukewarm water
beaten egg or milk to glaze
sesame seeds, poppy seeds or grated cheese for topping

❶ Sift the flour and salt together. Add sugar, milk powder and yeast and mix.

❷ Rub in margarine until mixture resembles fine breadcrumbs.

❸ Add lukewarm water and mix to a soft dough. Turn onto a lightly floured surface and knead for about 10 minutes, until the dough is smooth and elastic.

❹ Place dough in an oiled bowl and cover; allow to rest for 20 minutes.

❺ Knock down dough and divide into 15 equal pieces. Roll each piece into a ball, or shape into long sausages.

❻ Using a rolling pin, roll each ball of dough into a long oval and roll up tightly, like a Swiss roll. Place breadroll, with seam at bottom, on a greased baking tray.

❼ Cover with oiled plastic wrap and allow to rise in a warm place until double in size – 30–40 minutes.

❽ Brush with beaten egg or milk and sprinkle with sesame seeds, poppy seeds or grated cheese.

❾ Bake in a preheated oven at 200 °C (400 °F) for 15–20 minutes.

Makes 15

VARIATIONS

SPECIAL KITKE TREAT

1 Follow recipe for soft rolls. After first rising, knock down dough and divide into two equal pieces.

2 Roll each piece into a 40 cm strand and cross strands in the middle.

3 Take bottom left piece over to top right.

4 Plait the four strands until all the dough has been used. Seal ends together well. Leave to rise in a warm place until double in size – 30–40 minutes. Brush with beaten egg or milk and sprinkle with poppy seeds.

5 Bake in a preheated oven at 200 °C (400 °F) for 20–25 minutes.

CROWN LOAF

Place round rolls in a 22 cm loose-bottomed cake tin and sprinkle each with different seeds or cheese. Poppy seeds and sesame seeds are popular for topping bread and rolls, and for use in cakes and biscuits.

> **TIP**
>
> *The dough will be sticky when you start kneading, but will soon become smooth and satiny. It is properly kneaded when the impression made by a finger remains.*

WHOLEWHEAT ROLLS

750 ml Snowflake Nutty Wheat (450 g)
750 ml Snowflake cake flour (420 g)
10 ml salt
10 g instant dry yeast (1 sachet)
15 ml brown sugar, honey or molasses
50 ml cooking oil
10 ml vinegar
about 500 ml lukewarm water
beaten egg or milk to glaze

❶ Sift flour and salt together. Add bran left behind in sieve.

❷ Add yeast and brown sugar to dry ingredients.

❸ Mix oil, vinegar and lukewarm water, add to dry ingredients, and mix to a soft dough, adding more water if necessary.

❹ Turn onto a lightly floured surface and knead for about 10 minutes, until the dough is smooth and elastic.

❺ Place dough in an oiled bowl, cover, and allow to rest for 20 minutes.

❻ Knock down the dough and divide into 18 equal pieces. Roll each piece into a ball and shape as desired.

❼ Place rolls on a greased baking tray, cover with oiled plastic wrap, and allow to rise until double in size – 30–40 minutes.

❽ Brush with beaten egg or milk and sprinkle with crushed wheat if desired.

❾ Bake in a preheated oven at 200 °C (400 °F) for 20–25 minutes.

Makes 18

> **TIP**
>
> *When baking breads with yeast, add a little vinegar to the dough to prevent the 'yeasty' smell that sometimes occurs, especially when too much yeast has been used.*

VARIATIONS

HAMBURGER ROLLS

Roll a piece of bread dough into a ball using the palm of the hand.

HOTDOG ROLLS

Using a rolling pin, roll the ball of dough into a long, flat oval and roll up tightly, like a Swiss roll.

CLOVER ROLLS

Divide ball of dough into three equal pieces. Roll each piece into a ball. Join the three balls together to form a triangle.

KNOT ROLLS

Roll ball of dough into a long sausage shape. Make a loop near one end. Thread the remaining piece through the loop and make a knot.

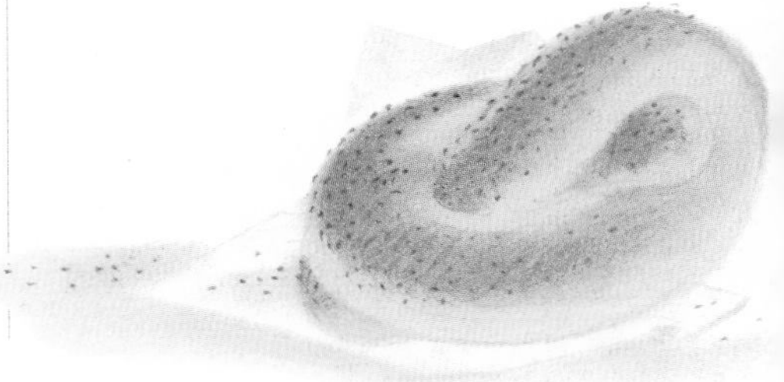

Clockwise from top left: Wholewheat Rolls, Soft Rolls, Special Kitke Treat and Crown Loaf.

8

BISCUITS AND RUSKS

THE WORD 'COOKIE' ORIGINATED FROM THE DUTCH WORD, *KOEKJE*. NOWADAYS, 'BISCUIT', WHICH IS DERIVED FROM THE OLD FRENCH WORD, *BESUIT*, A FLAT CAKE OF UNLEAVENED BREAD, IS MORE COMMONLY USED.
RUSKS ARE DRIED PORTIONS OF BREAD PREPARED FROM A DOUGH FLAVOURED WITH ANISEED OR RAISINS, FOR EXAMPLE. THEY ARE EASY TO MAKE AND AS TRADITIONAL AS BUTTERMILK, CONDENSED MILK AND MOSBOLLETJIES.

BISCUITS

Sweet or savoury biscuits are quick and easy to make at home.

According to the way in which they are made, biscuits can be divided into five categories:

Dropped biscuits

The dough is dropped or spooned onto the baking tray as it is very moist and sticky.

Rolled biscuits

The dough used for rolled biscuits is firm and can therefore be rolled out thinly, to a thickness of 3–5 mm, before being cut into shapes with biscuit cutters.

When rolling out, avoid having too much flour on your work surface, as the dough will lose its elasticity. Roll in one direction only to produce an even thickness. Roll sticky dough between two sheets of greaseproof paper.

Shaped biscuits

The dough is forced through a piping bag fitted with a nozzle, or is shaped by hand or using a biscuit maker. The dough must not be too soft or it will not hold its form. It may be chilled a while before baking to preserve its shape.

Refrigerator biscuits

The dough is shaped into long sausage forms and chilled in the refrigerator before being cut into slices, arranged on a baking tray, and baked.

Bars or slices

In texture, these resemble cakes, and are baked in cake tins and, once cooled, cut into bars or slices.

Hints on making biscuits

- Ingredients used for making biscuits should be kept at room temperature.
- The resulting number of biscuits will depend on the thickness of the dough when rolled out and on the size of the cookie cutter.
- The amount of liquid required will depend on the moisture content of the flour.
- Grease baking trays to prevent biscuits from sticking to the tray during baking. Place delicate mixtures on greaseproof paper or rice paper. Baking trays may also be dusted with flour after greasing.
- Remember that most biscuit mixtures spread during baking. When placing mixture on tray, leave sufficient room for spreading.
- Preheat oven before baking.
- Bake biscuits on the middle or top shelf of the oven.
- Once the baking tray is in the oven, ensure that there is space on either side of it, so that the warm air can circulate.
- If using a conventional oven it is best to bake one sheet of cookies at a time. If more than one baking tray is placed in the oven at a time, rotate the baking trays half-way through the baking process.
- Biscuits usually bake quickly. A moderate temperature is normally used over a short baking time. Use a timer and check the biscuits frequently to prevent browning or burning.
- Biscuits will be soft when removed from the oven, but will harden during cooling. The longer you bake biscuits, the harder they will become.

Cooling and storing biscuits

Using a spatula, lift biscuits from baking tray immediately after removing from oven to prevent further cooking. Place on a wire rack to cool.

Biscuits should be cooled completely before being stored in an airtight container, which will prevent them from becoming soft. Soft and crisp biscuits should be stored separately. If biscuits become soft, place in a cool oven at 150 °C (300 °F) for 5 minutes to restore crispness.

Hard biscuits can be successfully frozen for 2–3 months. Place cold biscuits in a plastic bag or container and place in deep-freeze. Allow biscuits to defrost at room temperature.

FLORENTINES

125 g butter
200 ml sugar (160 g)
50 ml golden syrup
125 ml Snowflake cake flour (70 g)
200 ml mixed peel (120 g)
200 ml chopped glacé cherries (120 g)
150 ml nibbed almonds (100 g)
75 ml flaked almonds (50 g)
100 g dark cooking chocolate

❶ Melt butter, sugar and syrup together and bring to the boil.

❷ Remove from heat and stir in flour, fruit and nuts.

❸ Place teaspoonfuls of mixture on a lightly greased baking tray, leaving enough space for spreading.

❹ Bake in preheated oven at 160 °C (325 °F) for 10–12 minutes.

❺ Remove from oven and smooth rough edges with a spatula. When biscuits feel more firm, lift gently from tray; turn onto a wire rack to cool.

❻ Melt chocolate in a bowl over hot water and cool until slightly thickened. Spread base of cold biscuits with chocolate. When almost set, create a wavy effect in the chocolate using a fork. Keep refrigerated.

Makes 50

Florentines.

PECAN BISCUITS

125 g butter or margarine
250 ml Snowflake self-raising flour (140 g)
125 ml chopped pecan nuts (50 g)
3 ml vanilla essence
50 ml icing sugar (25 g)
icing sugar for dusting

❶ Mix together all ingredients, except icing sugar for dusting.

❷ Shape into small balls and place on a greased baking tray. Press down lightly with a fork.

❸ Bake in a preheated oven at 160 °C (325 °F) for 25 minutes. Remove from oven and, while still hot, dust with icing sugar. Cool and store in an airtight container.

Makes 20

CINNAMON SNACKERS

125 g margarine
100 ml brown sugar (80 g)
1 egg
5 ml vanilla essence
300 ml Snowflake brown bread meal (170 g)

TOPPING
50 ml brown sugar (40 g)
5 ml cinnamon

❶ Cream the margarine and sugar together. Add egg and essence and beat until light and fluffy.

❷ Add sifted flour and mix to form a soft dough.

❸ For topping: Mix the sugar and cinnamon together.

❹ Shape dough into balls and roll in topping.

❺ Place balls on a baking tray and press down lightly with a fork. Bake in a preheated oven at 180 °C (350 °F) for 10–12 minutes. Store biscuits in an airtight container.

Makes 20

CHOCOLATE GINGER BISCUITS

125 g margarine
200 ml brown sugar (160 g)
1 egg
375 ml Snowflake brown bread meal (210 g)
10 ml baking powder
50 ml cocoa powder
125 ml finely chopped preserved ginger
30 g dark cooking chocolate

❶ Cream margarine and sugar well. Add egg and beat until light and fluffy.

❷ Sift the flour, baking powder and cocoa powder together and add, with bran left behind in sieve, to the creamed mixture.

❸ Add ginger and knead until mixture forms a soft dough.

❹ Shape teaspoonfuls of mixture into balls and place on lightly greased baking trays. Press the biscuits lightly with a fork. Allow room for spreading.

❺ Bake in a preheated oven at 180 °C (350 °F) for 12–15 minutes. Turn onto a wire rack to cool.

❻ Melt the chocolate and drizzle over the cold biscuits. Store in an airtight container.

Makes 30

TIP

Bake biscuits in a baking tray to ensure even browning, which is not always possible in a deeper baking tin.

CRISPY BISCUITS

125 g margarine
100 ml sugar (80 g)
1 egg
250 ml Snowflake brown bread meal (140 g)
10 ml baking powder
150 ml sultanas (90 g)
300 ml lightly crushed cornflakes (60 g)

❶ Beat margarine and sugar together. Add egg and beat well, until mixture is light and fluffy.

❷ Sift the flour and baking powder together, adding bran left behind in sieve to creamed mixture.

❸ Add sultanas and mix well.

❹ Drop teaspoonfuls of mixture into cornflakes and roll lightly to coat. Place on lightly greased baking tray. Allow room for spreading.

❺ Bake in a preheated oven at 180 °C (350 °F) for 20 minutes. Cool on a wire rack and store in an airtight container.

Makes 24

TIPS

For freshly baked biscuits at a moment's notice, freeze uncooked biscuits on trays. Once frozen, place in plastic bags, seal and freeze for 3 months. Defrost and bake as directed.

Undecorated biscuits that are starting to go soft can be crisped up in a hot oven. Place the biscuits on a baking tray and bake at 190 °C (375 °F) for 5 minutes.

From top: Crispy Biscuits, Pecan Biscuits, Chocolate Ginger Biscuits and Cinnamon Snackers.

ROMANY CREAMS

250 g butter
250 ml sugar (200 g)
500 ml Snowflake cake flour (280 g)
5 ml baking powder
2 ml salt
375 ml desiccated coconut (120 g)
30 ml cocoa powder
125 ml boiling water

FILLING
125 ml sugar (100 g)
15 ml butter
125 ml fresh cream
65 ml milk
5 ml vanilla essence
about 400 ml icing sugar (about 200 g)
50 g cooking chocolate, melted, optional

1. Cream butter and sugar together until light and fluffy.
2. Sift flour, baking powder and salt and add, with coconut, to creamed mixture. Mix well.
3. Dissolve cocoa powder in boiling water and add, mixing well.
4. Roll into balls or place teaspoonfuls on a greased baking tray. Bake in a preheated oven at 180 °C (350 °F) for 10–12 minutes.
5. For filling: Caramelize sugar and butter in a large saucepan.
6. Remove from heat and add cream and heated milk. Add essence and enough icing sugar to make a spreading consistency. Mix with melted chocolate if desired.
7. Sandwich pairs of biscuits together with filling.

Makes about 30 double biscuits

TIP

Keep unfilled biscuits in a container and, before serving, simply join two biscuits together with melted cooking chocolate.

BISCUITS FOR BISCUIT MAKER

250 g butter
125 ml sugar (100 g)
2 eggs
10 ml vanilla essence
625 ml Snowflake cake flour (350 g)
10 ml baking powder
2 ml salt

1. Cream butter and sugar together.
2. Add eggs one at a time, beating well after each addition. Add essence.
3. Sift dry ingredients together and add to creamed mixture. Mix well.
4. Place dough in biscuit maker and press onto a greased baking tray.
5. Bake in a preheated oven at 180 °C (350 °F) for 10 minutes. Cool and store in an airtight container.

Makes about 80

VARIATIONS

Substitute the 10 ml vanilla essence with 10 ml orange essence.

CHOCOLATE BISCUITS

Add 30 ml cocoa powder to dry ingredients.

TIP

If no biscuit maker is available, roll teaspoonfuls of dough in your hands, place on a greased baking tray, and press lightly with a fork.

SEMOLINA BISCUITS

200 g butter or margarine
65 ml castor sugar (55 g)
500 ml Snowflake cake flour (280 g)
250 ml semolina (160 g)
2 ml salt
65 ml milk
castor sugar

1. Cream butter and sugar until light.
2. Sift dry ingredients together and knead lightly into butter mixture. Add milk if necessary.
3. Turn onto a floured board and roll out to a thickness of 5 mm. Cut into rounds with a cookie cutter and prick with a fork.
4. Place on a greased baking tray and bake in a preheated oven at 180 °C (350 °F) for 15–20 minutes.
5. Sprinkle with castor sugar. Store in an airtight container.

Makes 50

VARIATION

For a lighter biscuit, substitute 50 ml cake flour with cornflour.

GINGERSNAPS

125 g margarine
250 ml sugar (200 g)
1 egg
125 ml ginger syrup
625 ml Snowflake cake flour (350 g)
5 ml bicarbonate of soda
8 ml ground cinnamon
5 ml ground ginger

1. Beat margarine and sugar together.
2. Add egg, beating well until light and fluffy. Mix in syrup.
3. Sift dry ingredients together, add to egg mixture and knead well to form a dough. Refrigerate for 1 hour.
4. Roll out on a lightly floured surface to a thickness of about 4 mm. Cut with a cookie cutter and place on a greased baking tray.
5. Bake in a preheated oven at 180 °C (350 °F) for 10 minutes. Cool and store in an airtight container.

Makes about 40

TIP

Crumble gingersnaps and use to add extra flavour and thickening to gravy in meat dishes.

Clockwise from top left: Romany Creams, Semolina Biscuits, Gingersnaps, Caramel Biscuits and Biscuits for Biscuit Maker.

CARAMEL BISCUITS

200 g butter or margarine
165 ml sugar (130 g)
380 g can caramel
5 ml caramel essence
750 ml Snowflake cake flour (420 g)
10 ml baking powder
3 ml salt

❶ Cream butter and sugar together until light and fluffy.

❷ Add caramel and essence and beat well.

❸ Sift dry ingredients together and knead well into caramel mixture.

❹ Roll into small balls, place on ungreased baking sheets and flatten with a fork.

❺ Bake in a preheated oven at 180 °C (350 °F) for 10–15 minutes. Turn onto a wire rack to cool.

Makes about 50

TIP

These biscuits burn easily, so keep a careful watch, being sure to check them underneath, too.

VIENNESE BISCUITS

250 g butter
65 ml castor sugar (55 g)
3 ml vanilla essence
440 ml Snowflake cake flour (245 g)
65 ml cornflour (30 g)
2 ml salt
icing sugar

❶ Beat butter and sugar together well. Add essence.

❷ Sift the flour, cornflour and salt together and blend into mixture until it is of a soft consistency.

❸ Spoon into piping bag fitted with a fluted tube.

❹ Pipe stars, straight lengths or other shapes onto lightly greased oven trays.

❺ Bake at 180 °C (350 °F) for 12–15 minutes, or until light gold in colour.

❻ Dust lightly with icing sugar before serving. Store in an airtight container.

Makes about 40

Variations

Dip one end of each biscuit into melted dark chocolate.

Dip one end of each biscuit into Granadilla Icing (page 66).

Use a star nozzle to make star-shaped biscuits. When cool, join together with Orange Icing; dust with icing sugar before serving.

Orange Icing

5 ml grated orange rind
25 ml orange juice
60 g soft butter
250 ml icing sugar (130 g)
Combine ingredients and beat until smooth.

Tip

To pipe biscuits: Hold piping bag upright, close to baking tray. Press gently to shape biscuit. Turn nozzle to complete shaping and lift sharply.

COCONUT BISCUITS

250 g butter
250 ml sugar (200 g)
3 egg whites
500 ml desiccated coconut (160 g)
125 ml sprinkle nuts (75 g)
2 ml grated lemon rind
750 ml Snowflake cake flour (420 g)

TOPPING
1 egg white, lightly beaten
150 ml coconut (50 g)
65 ml sugar (50 g)

❶ Cream butter and sugar together.

❷ Beat egg whites until stiff and fold in coconut, nuts and lemon rind. Fold egg white mixture into sugar mixture.

❸ Sift flour and mix thoroughly into creamed ingredients.

❹ Make rolls 30 mm in diameter and chill in refrigerator until firm.

❺ For topping: Brush rolls with egg white. Mix coconut and sugar and sprinkle over rolls.

❻ Cut into slices 7 mm thick. Place on a greased baking tray and bake in a preheated oven at 180 °C (350 °F) for 12–15 minutes. Turn onto a wire rack to cool. Store in an airtight container.

Makes 80

Tips

To brown desiccated coconut: Place fine coconut on greaseproof paper on a baking tray. Place in a cool oven and brown slowly. Allow to cool before using.

Unbroken egg yolks can be stored in the refrigerator covered with water. Drain off water before using.

Variation

Substitute sprinkle nuts with 100 ml crunchy peanut butter.

PINWHEEL BISCUITS

60 g butter
375 ml sugar (300 g)
2 egg yolks
5 ml vanilla essence
4 x 250 ml Snowflake cake flour (560 g)
15 ml baking powder
1 ml salt
100 ml milk
50 ml cocoa powder
50 ml water

❶ Beat butter and sugar together. Add egg yolks and beat well. Add essence.

❷ Sift flour, baking powder and salt together and add, with milk, to creamed mixture. Mix to a stiff dough. Add more milk if required.

❸ Divide mixture in two. Mix cocoa powder and water until smooth and add to one portion.

❹ Sprinkle work surface lightly with flour. Roll out mixtures separately, to a thickness of 3 mm; place one on top of the other and roll up.

❺ Seal in plastic wrap and refrigerate until firm.

❻ Cut 5 mm thick slices and place on greased baking trays.

❼ Bake in a preheated oven at 180 °C (350 °F) for 12–15 minutes.

❽ Turn onto a wire rack to cool. Store in an airtight container.

Makes 40, depending on size

Tip

Flour surface to make sure that the dough is not sticky when rolling up.

Clockwise from top right: Coconut Biscuits, Pinwheel Biscuits and Viennese Biscuits.

FRUIT SLICES

250 ml Snowflake self-raising flour (140 g)
5 ml mixed spice
125 ml castor sugar (105 g)
250 ml fruit cake mix (150 g)
125 ml desiccated coconut (40 g)
125 ml choc bits (100 g)
2 eggs, beaten
100 g butter, melted

ORANGE ICING
375 ml icing sugar (200 g)
5 ml soft butter
about 30 ml orange juice

❶ Combine sifted dry ingredients, sugar, fruit, coconut and choc bits.

❷ Stir in eggs and butter. Spoon and press mixture evenly into a greased 20 cm x 24 cm rectangular tin.

❸ Bake in a preheated oven at 180 °C (350 °F) for 20–25 minutes.

❹ Leave to cool for 15 minutes.

❺ For icing: Sift icing sugar, add butter and orange juice and mix until smooth. Spread icing over and leave to cool in tin before cutting into slices. Store in an airtight container.

Makes about 30

TIP

These biscuits are rather brittle, and should therefore be cut carefully.

SHORTBREAD

500 g butter
250 ml icing sugar (130 g)
4 x 250 ml Snowflake cake flour (560 g)
65 ml cornflour (30 g)
1 ml salt

❶ Beat the butter and icing sugar together well.

❷ Add the sifted dry ingredients and mix well.

❸ Knead dough very well until smooth, then press flat into an ungreased 20 cm x 24 cm rectangular tin. Prick surface with a fork.

❹ Place in preheated oven at 140 °C (275 °F) for 30 minutes and reduce heat to 120 °C (250 °F) for another 1½–2 hours.

❺ Cut into fingers while still warm. Leave for a few minutes to cool, then turn out onto a wire rack. Store in an airtight container.

Makes about 30

VARIATION

Divide mixture into two and flatten each into a round shape on an ungreased baking tray using a 20 cm round cake tin as a guide. Use your thumb and forefinger to pinch a decorative border around the edge of the circle. Mark out 12 sections on the shortbread and prick each section with a fork.

TIP

Prick biscuits with a fork before baking. This will release moisture and ensure a crisp biscuit.

NUTTY WHEAT SHORTBREAD

250 g butter
250 ml icing sugar (130 g)
250 ml Snowflake cake flour (140 g)
125 ml cornflour (60 g)
2 ml salt
250 ml Snowflake Nutty Wheat (150 g)
castor sugar

❶ Beat butter and icing sugar together until light and fluffy.

❷ Add sifted dry ingredients except castor sugar to butter mixture. Add bran left in sieve.

❸ Rub in to form a stiff dough.

❹ Press into a 20 cm x 24 cm rectangular tin. Prick with a fork and bake in a preheated oven at 160 °C (325 °F) for 45 minutes.

❺ Leave to cool in pan before cutting into bars. Dust with castor sugar. Store in an airtight container.

Makes 35

CARAMEL SHORTBREAD

SHORTBREAD
125 g butter
125 ml castor sugar (105 g)
250 ml Snowflake cake flour (140 g)
25 ml cornflour
2 ml salt

FUDGE LAYER
75 g butter
50 ml golden syrup
397 g can condensed milk
125 ml castor sugar (105 g)

CHOCOLATE TOPPING
150 g dark chocolate

❶ For shortbread: Beat butter and sugar together until light and fluffy.

❷ Sift the flour, cornflour and salt together and rub into butter and sugar mixture until a stiff dough is formed.

❸ Press into a greased 20 cm x 24 cm rectangular tin. Prick with a fork and bake in a preheated oven at 180 °C (350 °F) for 10 minutes. Reduce heat to 160 °C (325 °F) and bake a further 10 minutes.

❹ For fudge layer: Boil all ingredients in a saucepan for about 5 minutes, until thick. Beat constantly to prevent burning. Spread over baked shortbread and leave to cool until set.

❺ For chocolate topping: Melt the chocolate in top of double boiler over hot water and spread over fudge layer.

❻ Cut shortbread into squares just before chocolate hardens. Store in an airtight container.

Makes about 50

Clockwise from top left: Crunchies, Caramel Shortbread, Fruit Slices, Nutty Wheat Shortbread and Shortbread.

CRUNCHIES

200 g margarine
7 ml bicarbonate of soda
15 ml golden syrup
500 ml rolled oats (160 g)
250 ml Snowflake white bread flour (140 g)
250 ml castor sugar (210 g)
250 ml desiccated coconut (80 g)

❶ Melt margarine and add bicarbonate of soda and syrup.

❷ Mix dry ingredients together and combine with the melted mixture.

❸ Press into a 20 cm x 24 cm rectangular tin and bake in a preheated oven at 160 °C (325 °F) for 40–45 minutes, until golden brown.

❹ Remove from oven and cut into squares while still warm. Store in an airtight container.

Makes about 25

VARIATIONS

Substitute the white bread flour with cake flour or brown bread meal.

Substitute golden syrup with maple syrup.

TIP

Crunchies will store well in the deep-freeze for 6 months.

PEANUT CARAMEL BARS

125 g butter or margarine
125 ml sugar (100 g)
1 egg yolk
315 ml Snowflake cake flour (180 g)
2 ml baking powder
25 ml custard powder
2 ml salt

TOPPING
100 ml soft brown sugar (80 g)
30 ml golden syrup
100 g butter or margarine
125 ml roasted unsalted peanuts (75 g)

❶ Beat butter and sugar together. Add egg yolk and mix until light and fluffy.

❷ Add dry ingredients and mix to form a stiff dough.

❸ Press mixture into a well-greased 20 cm x 24 cm rectangular tin.

❹ Bake in a preheated oven at 180 °C (350 °F) for 20–25 minutes, or until golden brown.

❺ For topping: Place brown sugar, golden syrup and butter in a saucepan. Stir over a low heat until butter has melted and sugar has dissolved. Simmer gently for 5 minutes. Stir in roughly chopped nuts.

❻ Remove from the oven, spread with prepared topping mixture, and return to the oven for a further 5 minutes. Leave to cool in the tin, then cut into bars. Store in an airtight container.

Makes about 25

TIP

Butter gives a superior flavour and is responsible for the richness and shortness of the biscuit.

RUSKS

Rusks can be made from cake flour or wholewheat flour, which is the more popular because of its health benefit. The rusk dough is shaped into small balls, which are arranged next to one another. Butter or margarine can be used, but butter gives a better flavour than margarine. However, if rusks are to be kept for a long time, use margarine.

After baking, place rusks on a wire rack and break in half using two forks. Some rusks may need to be cut with a knife. Place rusks on a wire rack on an ungreased baking tray and dry out overnight in the warming drawer of the oven. Alternatively, dry them in the oven at the lowest temperature – about 50 °C (100 °F) – until completely dried out. (Place a spoon in the oven door to allow moisture to escape.) Check rusks constantly to prevent them from burning or becoming too brown. Turn them over and dry on the other side as well. Cool completely before storing in an airtight container. Rusks can be stored this way for up to 3 months.

BRAN RUSKS

800 ml boiling water
375 ml sugar (300 g)
350 g margarine
3 eggs, beaten
7 x 250 ml Snowflake self-raising flour (1 kg)
15 ml baking powder
10 ml salt
5 ml cream of tartar
500 ml Snowflake digestive bran (60 g)

❶ Combine boiling water, sugar and margarine. Stir until margarine has melted. Allow mixture to cool and add eggs.

❷ Sift flour, baking powder, salt and cream of tartar together, and add to egg mixture.

❸ Add digestive bran and stir until well mixed. (Mixture will be runny.)

❹ Pour into three greased 23 cm loaf tins.

❺ Bake in a preheated oven at 180 °C (350 °F) for 1 hour.

❻ Leave in tins for a few minutes to cool. Turn out onto a wire rack to cool completely. Cut each loaf into seven thick slices and then divide each slice into three again. (Use an electric knife, if possible, to prevent breaking.)

❼ Dry out overnight in warming drawer, or in a very cool oven.

Makes 72, depending on size

WHOLEWHEAT RUSKS

875 ml Snowflake cake flour (500 g)
875 ml Snowflake Nutty Wheat (525 g)
50 ml baking powder
5 ml salt
315 ml sugar (250 g)
500 g butter
500 ml buttermilk

❶ Sift dry ingredients together. Add bran left behind in sieve. Add sugar.

❷ Melt butter and add buttermilk. Mix into dry ingredients.

❸ Shape dough into balls and place in a large, greased oven pan.

❹ Bake in a preheated oven at 180 °C (350 °F) for 60 minutes.

❺ Break into pieces and dry out in the warming drawer overnight, or in a very cool oven.

Makes 40, depending on size

From top: Wholewheat Rusks, Bran Rusks and Peanut Caramel Bars.

HEALTH RUSKS

500 g margarine
375 ml soft brown sugar (300 g)
2 eggs, beaten
500 ml buttermilk
7 x 250 ml Snowflake self-raising flour (1 kg)
15 ml baking powder
5 ml salt
4 x 250 ml All Bran Flakes (200 g)
625 ml Snowflake digestive bran (75 g)
150 ml sunflower seeds (90 g)
125 ml seedless raisins (75 g)

❶ Melt margarine and sugar together. Leave to cool.

❷ Add eggs and buttermilk.

❸ Sift flour, baking powder and salt together. Add All Bran Flakes, digestive bran, sunflower seeds and raisins. Add egg mixture.

❹ Shape into balls and place into a large, greased oven pan.

❺ Bake in a preheated oven at 180 °C (350 °F) for 45–50 minutes.

❻ Turn out onto a wire rack to cool slightly, break open while still warm, and leave to cool further. Dry out overnight in the warming drawer, or in a very cool oven.

Makes 60, depending on size

TIPS

Do not cut these rusks with a knife as they will break easily.

Place spoon in oven door while drying out to allow air to circulate.

CONDENSED MILK RUSKS

2,5 kg Snowflake cake flour
20 ml salt
400 ml sugar (320 g)
20 g instant dry yeast (2 sachets)
2 eggs, beaten
1,5 litres lukewarm water
250 g margarine or butter, melted
397 g can condensed milk

❶ Sift flour and salt together. Add sugar and dry yeast.

❷ Mix eggs, lukewarm water, margarine and condensed milk together, add to dry ingredients, and mix to a soft dough.

❸ Knead dough for about 10 minutes, until smooth and elastic.

❹ Place dough in an oiled bowl, cover and allow to rise for 20 minutes.

❺ Knock down the dough and shape into balls. Place in large greased oven pans, cover with oiled plastic wrap, and leave to rise in a warm place until double in size – about 30 minutes.

❻ Bake in a preheated oven at 180 °C (350 °F) for 1 hour.

❼ Turn out onto a wire rack to cool slightly, break open while still warm, and leave to cool further. Dry out overnight in the warming drawer, or in a very cool oven at 50 °C (100 °F).

Makes 200, depending on size

TIP

Cut dough with a pair of kitchen scissors and shape into balls.

BUTTERMILK RUSKS 1

2,5 kg Snowflake self-raising flour
10 ml salt
625 ml sugar (500 g)
15 ml whole aniseed, optional
750 g margarine
1,5 litres buttermilk
3 eggs, beaten

❶ Sift flour and salt together. Add sugar and aniseed. Rub in margarine until mixture resembles breadcrumbs.

❷ Mix buttermilk and eggs together, add to above mixture and mix well.

❸ Shape dough into balls and place in large, greased oven pans.

❹ Bake in a preheated oven at 160 °C (325 °F) for 20 minutes and then reduce heat to 150 °C (300 °F) for a further 30 minutes.

❺ Turn out onto a wire rack to cool slightly, break open while still warm, and leave to cool further. Dry out overnight in the warming drawer, or in a very cool oven at 50 °C (100 °F).

Makes 200, depending on size

TIP

If rusks brown too quickly, cover with aluminium foil to prevent further browning.

BUTTERMILK RUSKS 2

1,5 kg Snowflake self-raising flour
3 ml salt
10 ml cream of tartar
500 g butter
430 ml sugar (350 g)
500 ml buttermilk

❶ Sift dry ingredients together.

❷ Melt butter and sugar together and add, together with buttermilk, to dry ingredients. Mix well.

❸ Shape into balls and place in a large greased oven pan.

❹ Bake in a preheated oven at 180 °C (350 °F) for 1 hour.

❺ Turn out onto a wire rack to cool slightly, break open while still warm, and leave to cool further. Dry out overnight in the warming drawer, or in a very cool oven at 50 °C (100 °F).

Makes 40, depending on size

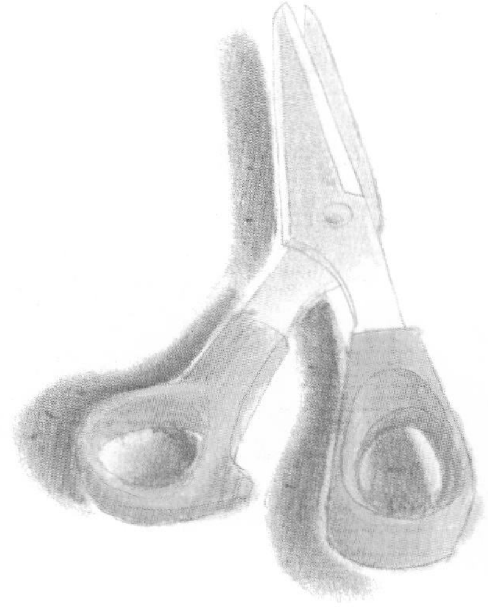

Clockwise from top left: Buttermilk Rusks 2, Condensed Milk Rusks, Buttermilk Rusks 1 and Health Rusks.

9

Desserts

'Dessert' is derived from a French word meaning 'to clear the table', a tradition still practised in restaurants before the sweet course is served. No matter whether it is called 'dessert', 'pudding' or 'sweets', this part of the meal is something special – for some, the best part! The recipes in this chapter cater for every taste, and include baked and batter puddings, iced desserts, fruit puddings and a cold mousse.

VANILLA AND CHOCOLATE ICE-CREAM

250 ml sugar (200 g)
65 ml Snowflake cake flour (35 g)
2 ml salt
750 ml milk
2 eggs
15 ml vanilla essence
250 ml fresh cream, beaten
100 g plain chocolate

❶ Mix sugar, flour and salt in a heavy-based saucepan. Add milk; bring to boil. Boil for 5 minutes while beating.

❷ Add a little mixture to beaten eggs. Pour into milk and boil until thickened – for 3–5 minutes. Leave to cool.

❸ Add 10 ml of essence and the cream to cooled custard. Divide mixture into two and add 5 ml essence to one mixture for vanilla ice-cream.

❹ Melt chocolate and add to second mixture. Freeze mixtures separately. Serve with chocolate or caramel sauce once frozen.

Makes 1 litre

Variation

Substitute 15 ml vanilla essence with 10 ml peppermint essence and a few drops of green food colouring.

TUILES

100 g butter
100 ml castor sugar (85 g)
150 ml Snowflake cake flour (85 g)
1 egg white

❶ Cream butter and sugar together. Add flour and mix well.

❷ Lightly beat egg white and add to creamed mixture.

❸ Place about two teaspoonfuls of mixture on a greased baking tray. Use a spatula or spoon to spread evenly in a large circle.

❹ Bake in a preheated oven at 180 °C (350 °F) for 6–7 minutes, until just starting to brown. Bake only four at a time as they must be shaped immediately after baking, before they set.

❺ Remove carefully with a spatula and place each over the bottom of an inverted glass, pressing lightly. Cool.

❻ Fill with Ice-cream (this page) or Custard (page 98) and serve on top of puréed fruit.

Makes 24

Tips

These biscuits start getting hard and crisp very quickly, so bake only a few at a time.

They can be made two days ahead and stored in an airtight container.

APPLE AND PEAR CRUMBLE

385 g can pie apples
410 g can pears, drained
125 ml raisins (75 g)
5 ml ground cinnamon
5 ml ground ginger
200 ml Snowflake cake flour (110 g)
125 ml soft brown sugar (100 g)
65 g margarine

❶ Mix the apples, pears, raisins, cinnamon and ginger together; spoon into a 23 cm ovenproof pie dish.

❷ Sift flour and add sugar. Rub in margarine until mixture resembles fine breadcrumbs. Sprinkle over fruit.

❸ Bake in a preheated oven at 180 °C (350 °F) for 30 minutes. Serve with cold, thick fresh cream, custard or ice-cream.

Serves 4-6

GRANADILLA CREAM

40 ml cake flour (20 g)
125 ml castor sugar (105 g)
10 ml gelatine
200 ml water
250 ml apricot juice
115 g can granadilla pulp
170 g can evaporated milk, chilled

❶ Combine flour, sugar, gelatine and water in a saucepan. Simmer until mixture thickens, stirring constantly.

❷ Stir in juice and granadilla pulp. Refrigerate until mixture starts to set.

❸ Beat milk until fluffy and fold into granadilla mixture.

❹ Pour into serving glasses and refrigerate until set. Serve with cream or ice-cream.

Serves 4

Variation

Substitute apricot juice with orange juice.

Clockwise from top left: Apple and Pear Crumble, Granadilla Cream and Tuile with Vanilla Ice-cream.

BASIC PANCAKES

500 ml Snowflake cake flour (280 g)
2 ml salt
2 eggs
500 ml water
5 ml brandy or lemon juice
cinnamon sugar

❶ Sift flour and salt together.

❷ Whisk eggs and water together and add to flour. Add brandy, beating constantly until smooth.

❸ Leave batter to stand for at least an hour before using. If batter is too thick, add more water.

❹ Lightly oil a heavy-based frying pan and heat. Pour batter into pan; fry until lightly browned on both sides.

❺ Sprinkle with cinnamon sugar and roll up.

Makes 15–20, depending on pan size

VARIATION

CRÊPES
Make crêpes using 250 ml flour to 2 eggs. Serve with Orange Sauce (this page).

TIPS

Keep pancakes warm by placing over boiling water.

To freeze, allow pancakes to cool, then stack between sheets of greaseproof paper. Wrap in foil and freeze for up to 2 months. To use, thaw and peel off one by one.

To keep crêpes warm, brush with melted butter and place in oven.

Batter can be frozen.

Custard Filling

50 ml custard powder (25 g)
500 ml milk
25 ml sugar (20 g)
440 g can pineapple pieces, drained
25 ml margarine
5 ml vanilla essence

❶ Mix custard powder with a little milk. Heat rest of milk and sugar.

❷ Stir custard mixture into milk. Cut pineapple into smaller pieces and add. Cook until thickened.

❸ Remove from heat and stir in margarine and essence.

❹ Fill pancakes.

Orange Sauce

125 ml sugar (100 g)
200 ml orange juice
100 g margarine
10 ml grated orange rind
15 ml cornflour
25 ml brandy

❶ Heat sugar, orange juice, margarine and orange rind. Thicken with cornflour and leave to boil a few minutes.

❷ Heat brandy in a small saucepan (do not boil), pour over sauce, ignite and leave until flames subside.

VARIATION

Substitute brandy with Grand Marnier or Tia Maria.

WHOLEWHEAT PANCAKES

250 ml Snowflake cake flour (140 g)
250 ml Snowflake Nutty Wheat (150 g)
3 ml salt
2 eggs
250 ml milk
375 ml water
50 ml oil
15 ml brandy or lemon juice
cinnamon sugar

❶ Sift flour, Nutty Wheat and salt together. Add bran left behind in sieve.

❷ Whisk eggs, milk and water together and add gradually to the dry ingredients, beating constantly.

❸ Add oil and brandy and beat well.

❹ Allow batter to stand, covered, for 1½ hours before using. If batter is too thick, add more water.

❺ Pour a little batter into a lightly oiled and heated heavy-based frying pan. Tip pan to allow mixture to coat base evenly. Fry for 1–2 minutes or until lightly browned.

❻ Turn pancake and fry the other side. Sprinkle with cinnamon sugar and roll up or fill with Almond Filling, and top with Strawberry Sauce.

Makes 15–20 depending on pan size

Almond Filling

125 ml sugar (100 g)
250 ml milk
65 ml Snowflake cake flour (35 g)
2 eggs, separated
65 ml nibbed almonds (40 g)
50 g margarine
5 ml vanilla essence
2 ml almond essence

Strawberry Sauce

410 g can strawberries in syrup
65 ml sugar (50 g)
15 ml cornflour

❶ For filling: Heat sugar, milk and flour together. Beat until smooth.

❷ Add some of the hot mixture to beaten egg yolks. Pour into hot mixture, beat well and cook until mixture starts to thicken.

❸ Remove from heat and add almonds, margarine and vanilla and almond essence.

❹ Beat egg whites until stiff and fold into mixture.

❺ For sauce: Heat strawberries with their syrup and the sugar. Thicken with cornflour and water paste and boil for a few minutes.

❻ Fill pancakes, and pour sauce over.

From top: Crépes with Orange Sauce, Wholewheat Pancakes with Almond Filling and Strawberry Sauce.

SEMOLINA PUDDING

500 ml milk
50 ml semolina (30 g)
20 ml margarine
1 egg, separated
2 ml grated lemon rind
50 ml castor sugar (40 g)

❶ Heat milk, add semolina, and simmer for approximately 5 minutes.

❷ Remove from heat and add margarine, egg yolk, lemon rind and 40 ml castor sugar.

❸ Beat egg white until soft peak stage. Fold into egg mixture and pour into a 20 cm round ovenproof dish.

❹ Sprinkle remaining castor sugar over and bake in a preheated oven at 180 °C (350 °F) for 20 minutes.

Serves 4

TIP

Never waste rind. Grate off before halving and squeezing the fruit; store in a covered container in the deep-freeze. Use in frozen state.

CHOCOLATE SELF-SAUCING PUDDING

50 g butter or margarine
200 ml castor sugar (170 g)
1 egg
250 ml Snowflake cake flour (140 g)
25 ml cocoa powder
15 ml baking powder
2 ml salt
200 ml milk

SYRUP
250 ml water
250 ml brown sugar (200 g)
25 ml cocoa powder
5 ml vanilla essence

❶ Cream butter and sugar. Add egg and beat until light and fluffy.

❷ Sift dry ingredients and add, alternately with milk, to butter mixture.

❸ Spoon mixture into a large ovenproof dish.

❹ For syrup: Mix all ingredients except essence in a saucepan, heat and stir until sugar has dissolved and mixture starts to boil. Add essence.

❺ Pour syrup over batter and bake in a preheated oven at 180 °C (350 °F) for 30 minutes.

❻ Serve with custard or fresh cream.

Serves 4–6

MERINGUE PUDDING

15 ml margarine
125 ml sugar (100 g)
2 eggs, separated
250 ml Snowflake cake flour (140 g)
5 ml baking powder
2 ml salt
500 ml milk
50 ml smooth apricot jam (65 g)
25 ml sugar for egg whites

❶ Cream the margarine and sugar together. Add egg yolks and beat until light and fluffy.

❷ Sift flour, baking powder and salt and add, alternately with 100 ml milk, to sugar mixture.

❸ Spoon into a greased ovenproof dish and bake in a preheated oven at 180 °C (350 °F) for 40 minutes.

❹ Remove from oven and pour remaining milk over pudding. Spread apricot jam over.

❺ Beat egg whites with 25 ml sugar until soft peak stage. Spread over pudding and bake for a further 15 minutes, until golden brown.

❻ Serve with custard.

Serves 6

LEMON PUDDING

125 ml Snowflake cake flour (70 g)
2 ml salt
200 ml sugar (160 g)
50 g butter or margarine
3 eggs, separated
10 ml grated lemon rind
60 ml lemon juice
250 ml milk

❶ Sift flour and salt together. Add sugar.

❷ Rub in butter until mixture resembles fine breadcrumbs.

❸ Beat in egg yolks, lemon rind, lemon juice and milk until smooth.

❹ Fold in stiffly beaten egg whites.

❺ Pour into a medium-sized, greased ovenproof dish and place in baking tin or roasting pan half-filled with water. Bake in a preheated oven at 180 °C (350 °F) for 35 minutes.

Serves 4

TIPS

Before grating lemon rind, dip grater into cold water. The rind will slip off the grater more easily.

When a small amount of lemon juice is needed, make a hole in the lemon with a skewer and squeeze out the amount required. Store lemon in the refrigerator.

To create a delicate texture, place a layer of newspaper under a dish standing in water during baking.

Clockwise from top left: Meringue Pudding, Chocolate Self-saucing Pudding, Semolina Pudding and Lemon Pudding.

PINEAPPLE UPSIDE-DOWN PUDDING

125 g butter
75 ml brown sugar (60 g)
440 g can pineapple rings
glacé cherries
pecan nuts
200 ml white sugar (160 g)
1 egg
375 ml Snowflake self-raising flour (210 g)
2 ml salt
125 ml milk

❶ Grease base of a 20 cm cake tin or medium-sized ovenproof dish.

❷ Cream 60 g of butter with brown sugar and spoon onto base of tin. Place pineapple rings on base and decorate with cherries and nuts.

❸ Cream the remaining butter with the white sugar. Add egg and beat until light and fluffy.

❹ Sift flour and salt together and add, alternately with milk, to egg mixture.

❺ Spoon mixture over fruit and bake in a preheated oven at 180 °C (350 °F) for 40–50 minutes.

❻ Turn out onto a serving dish and serve hot with ice-cream or cream.

Serves 6

TIP

If you are using an ovenproof dish, place extra pineapple rings around sides of dish.

PEACH STRUDEL

PASTRY
250 ml Snowflake cake flour (140 g)
2 ml salt
30 ml melted butter
1 egg yolk
about 65 ml lukewarm water
extra butter, melted

FILLING
15 g butter
125 ml fresh breadcrumbs (30 g)
410 g can peach slices in syrup, drained
100 ml sugar (80 g)
10 ml ground cinnamon
2 ml allspice
125 ml pitted raisins (75 g)

❶ For pastry: Sift flour and salt together. Make a well in centre and mix in half of melted butter.

❷ Mix egg yolk and water together and add to dry ingredients. Mix to form a soft dough. Beat until dough comes away from sides of bowl.

❸ Knead well, until smooth and elastic. Flatten dough and brush with remaining melted butter. Cover well and leave to stand at room temperature for at least 30 minutes or overnight if possible. Dough will become more elastic.

❹ Place dough on surface sprinkled with flour or on a large cotton cloth and roll out very thinly. Stretch while rolling out to a very thin rectangular shape of about 25 cm x 35 cm. Brush pastry with melted butter.

❺ For filling: Heat butter and fry breadcrumbs until crisp. Spread over pastry.

❻ Combine peach slices with sugar, cinnamon, allspice and raisins.

❼ Place filling on one edge of pastry. Starting from this end, roll up tightly.

❽ Place on greased baking tray and brush with remaining melted butter.

❾ Bake in a preheated oven at 190 °C (375 °F) for 30–35 minutes.

❿ Cut into diagonal slices; serve hot.

Serves 6

VARIATION

Substitute peaches with canned apples, cherries or apricots.

TIP

Freeze strudel unbaked. To bake, place, frozen, in a preheated oven and bake as directed in recipe, allowing an extra 15–20 minutes of baking time.

BAKED ROLY-POLY

500 ml Snowflake self-raising flour (280 g)
1 ml salt
125 g butter
2 eggs
50 ml milk
2 ml vanilla essence
80 ml smooth apricot jam (105 g)

SYRUP
375 ml boiling water
250 ml sugar (200 g)
30 ml butter

❶ Sift flour and salt together. Rub in butter until the mixture resembles breadcrumbs.

❷ Beat eggs, milk and essence, stir into flour, and mix to a soft dough.

❸ On floured surface, roll out dough to a thickness of 5 mm and a rectangular shape of about 22 cm x 25 cm. Spread with jam.

❹ Roll up as for Swiss roll, cut into slices of 2 cm, and place in a rectangular ovenproof dish.

❺ For syrup: Mix all ingredients together and pour over slices.

❻ Bake in a preheated oven at 180 °C (350 °F) for 30–45 minutes.

Serves 4–6

SPICY DUMPLINGS

250 ml Snowflake cake flour (140 g)
2 ml salt
5 ml bicarbonate of soda
15 ml margarine
1 egg, beaten
30 ml milk
15 ml smooth apricot jam

SYRUP
375 ml water
250 ml sugar (200 g)
5 ml ground cinnamon
5 ml ground ginger
2 ml ground nutmeg

❶ Sift flour, salt and bicarbonate of soda together. Rub in margarine.

❷ Add egg, milk and apricot jam and mix well.

❸ For syrup: Mix all ingredients together and bring to boil.

❹ Drop spoonfuls of dough into the boiling syrup. Cover and boil for 15 minutes. Do not remove the lid while cooking. Serve hot.

Serves 4

TRIFLE

1 Swiss roll (page 56)
smooth apricot jam
125 ml sherry
410 g can peach slices in syrup, drained
60 ml halved glacé cherries (40 g)
125 ml walnuts, optional (50 g)
1 quantity Confectioner's Custard (page 43)
125 ml fresh cream, whipped

❶ Cut cake into slices and place in serving dish. Sprinkle with sherry and leave to soak while preparing custard.

❷ Arrange fruit, cherries and nuts on soaked cake. Cover with custard. Extra fruit can be placed on top of cake if desired.

❸ Decorate with whipped cream, extra cherries and nuts. Chill for a few hours, or overnight if possible.

Serves 6–8

From top: Trifle and Peach Strudel.

BAKING FOR SPECIAL OCCASIONS

EASTER IS CELEBRATED IN DIFFERENT WAYS ALL OVER THE WORLD AND VARIOUS SPECIAL FOODS ARE ASSOCIATED WITH IT. FOR EXAMPLE, HOT CROSS BUNS, DECORATED WITH THE SYMBOLIC CROSS, ARE CUSTOMARILY EATEN ON GOOD FRIDAY. SPICE BUNS, WHICH ARE SIMILAR, ARE ALSO EATEN AT EASTER. CHRISTMAS IS USUALLY A TIME OF JOY AND EXCHANGING PRESENTS. MINCE PIES OR INDIVIDUAL CHRISTMAS CAKES ARE ALWAYS POPULAR GIFTS.

HOT CROSS BUNS

375 ml milk
60 g butter
4 x 250 ml Snowflake cake flour (560 g)
15 ml mixed spice
5 ml ground cinnamon
5 ml salt
65 ml castor sugar (55 g)
10 g instant dry yeast (1 sachet)
200 ml sultanas (120 g)
1 egg, beaten

FLOUR PASTE FOR CROSSES
125 ml Snowflake cake flour (70 g)
10 ml castor sugar
about 75 ml water

GLAZE
30 ml milk
30 ml castor sugar

❶ Heat milk and butter together and leave to cool slightly.

❷ Sift flour, spices and salt together. Add sugar, yeast and sultanas.

❸ Stir in warm milk and butter, and egg. Knead well until smooth – about 10 minutes. Cover and leave in a warm place for about 1 hour, or until dough has doubled in size.

❹ Knead a few minutes until smooth. Divide into 12 medium-sized balls and place on a greased baking tray. Cover and leave in a warm place for 10 minutes, or until the buns have risen.

❺ For crosses: Mix flour and sugar together and add enough water to form a smooth paste. Place the paste in a piping bag; using the small, plain tube fitting, make crosses on the buns.

❻ Bake in a preheated oven at 190 °C (375 °F) for 15–20 minutes.

❼ For glaze: Heat milk and sugar without boiling. Turn buns onto a wire rack and brush with hot glaze.

Makes 12

QUICK SPICE MUFFINS

These muffins are similar to hot cross buns, but do not have the same texture. They are popular all year round.

4 x 250 ml Snowflake cake flour (560 g)
25 ml baking powder
3 ml salt
15 ml mixed spice
5 ml cinnamon
200 g margarine
200 ml soft brown sugar (160 g)
500 ml fruit cake mix (300 g)
1 egg
375 ml milk

❶ Sift dry ingredients together.

❷ Rub in margarine until mixture resembles breadcrumbs.

❸ Add sugar and cake mix.

❹ Whisk egg and milk together and add to dry ingredients. Mix until flour is moistened; batter should still be lumpy.

❺ Spoon into greased muffin tins, filling each two-thirds full. Bake in a preheated oven at 190 °C (375 °F) for 20–25 minutes.

❻ Serve with butter.

Makes 24

POPPY SEED EASTER CAKE

200 g butter
375 ml sugar (300 g)
5 eggs, separated
750 ml Snowflake cake flour (420 g)
25 ml baking powder
250 ml orange juice
125 ml sherry
150 ml poppy seeds (90 g)
125 ml sugar (100 g)

❶ Cream butter and sugar together until light and fluffy.

❷ Add egg yolks and beat well.

❸ Add sifted flour and baking powder alternately with the orange juice. Add sherry.

❹ Gradually add the poppy seeds to mixture while beating well.

❺ In a separate bowl, whisk the egg whites and sugar until stiff. Fold egg whites into the poppy seed mixture.

❻ Pour mixture into a greased, deep, round or square 23 cm cake tin.

❼ Bake in a preheated oven at 160 °C (325 °F) for 1½ hours. Turn out onto a wire rack to cool.

TIP

For use in cakes, poppy seeds are often ground, or cooked in milk until soft. It is believed that the best poppy seeds, which are slate-blue in colour come from Holland. In some countries they are crushed for their oil, which is used as salad oil.

Clockwise from top: Hot Cross Buns, Quick Spice Muffins and Poppy Seed Easter Cake.

SIMNEL CAKE

Today, simnel cake is associated with Easter Sunday, the marzipan balls representing the 11 faithful disciples.

200 g butter or margarine
125 ml brown sugar (100 g)
3 eggs
750 ml fruit cake mix (500 g)
375 ml Snowflake cake flour (210 g)
5 ml ground cinnamon
5 ml ground mixed spice
3 ml ground nutmeg
2 ml salt
750 g marzipan
apricot jam for spreading

❶ Cream butter and sugar well.

❷ Add eggs, one at a time. Beat well until light and fluffy.

❸ Add fruit and sifted dry ingredients. Mix well.

❹ Grease and line a 18 cm x 7 cm round cake tin. Spread half of cake mixture onto base of tin.

❺ Roll out 250 g of marzipan and cut out an 18 cm circle. Place this over mixture in tin and cover it with remaining fruit mixture.

❻ Bake in a preheated oven at 150 °C (300 °F) for 2 hours, until lightly browned.

❼ Allow to cool in tin. Wrap in plastic wrap so that it is airtight, and store for at least a week.

❽ When ready to use, brush surface of cake with apricot jam and cover with a circle of marzipan. Crimp edges of marzipan and brush again with jam. Make marzipan balls and position them on surface.

❾ Grill a few minutes until browned. Decorate with fruit and ribbon if desired. Keep in an airtight container for up to 2 weeks.

TIP

Watch cake constantly while it is under the grill and turn it around when necessary. This will ensure even browning of the marzipan and prevent it from burning.

EASTER BISCUITS

500 ml Snowflake cake flour (280 g)
1 ml ground mixed spice
1 ml ground cinnamon
125 g butter
125 ml castor sugar (105 g)
65 ml currants (40 g)
2 ml lemon rind
1 egg, beaten
about 30 ml milk
castor sugar

❶ Sift dry ingredients together. Rub in butter until mixture resembles fine breadcrumbs.

❷ Add remaining ingredients except castor sugar and mix to a stiff dough.

❸ Roll out to a thickness of 3 mm. Cut rounds with a cookie cutter and place on a greased baking tray.

❹ Bake in a preheated oven at 180 °C (350 °F) for 15 minutes. Sprinkle with castor sugar.

❺ Cool on a wire rack and store in an airtight container.

Makes about 45

TIP

For a crisper biscuit, substitute half butter with lard.

NUTTY EASTER TREAT

DOUGH
4 x 250 ml Snowflake white bread flour (560 g)
125 ml castor sugar (105 g)
2 ml salt
10 g instant dry yeast (1 sachet)
200 ml lukewarm milk
100 g butter or margarine, melted
2 eggs, beaten

FILLING
125 ml coarsely chopped walnuts (50 g)
65 ml coarsely chopped pecan nuts (25 g)
65 ml coarsely chopped almonds (40 g)
60 g butter or margarine, melted
30 ml honey or golden syrup
15 ml ground cinnamon

TOPPING
Glacé Icing (page 67)
glazed fruit

❶ Sift flour, sugar and salt together. Add yeast.

❷ Add milk to dry ingredients with melted butter and eggs, to form a soft dough. Knead for 10 minutes, until smooth and elastic.

❸ Place dough in a greased plastic bag and allow to rise for about 30 minutes, until double in size.

❹ For filling: Mix nuts with remaining filling ingredients.

❺ Knock down the dough and allow to rise for a further 10 minutes.

❻ Flatten dough into a 45 cm x 30 cm rectangle. Spread with filling. Roll up from the long side.

❼ Join the ends of the roll together to form a circle. Using a pair of scissors, make 20 cuts into the circle, each three-quarters of the width of the dough. Turn each wedge on its side.

❽ Place on a greased baking tray and bake at 180 °C (350 °F) for 35 minutes, until golden brown.

❾ Pour the Glacé Icing over the warm ring and decorate with glazed fruit.

From top: Nutty Easter Treat, Simnel Cake and Easter Biscuits.

FRUIT CAKES

Rich fruit cakes should be made at least two months before Christmas to allow all the flavours to develop.

Lining the tin

To ensure a well-shaped cake, it is most important to line the cake tin correctly. Lining the tin protects the cake during the long cooking process, so the longer the cooking time, the heavier the lining should be. For a 20 cm square cake tin two layers of brown paper or two layers of greaseproof paper should be used. If baking for longer than 3 hours, the lining paper should stand a few centimetres above the edge of the tin to protect the top of the cake.

First cut the strips for the sides of the tin, then use the base of the tin as a guide for cutting the paper for the base.

Preparing cake mixture

Eggs and butter should be at room temperature. Add the sugar until just combined. Add the eggs one at a time and do not overmix. Add the fruit mixture to the creamed mixture and mix the ingredients well (rich fruit cakes do not contain any raising agent). Spoon the mixture carefully into the lined tin and level the top with a spatula.

When baking more than one cake at a time, the cooking time will be a little longer due to greater absorption of heat.

After removing the cake from the oven, leave it in the tin to cool completely. Then brush it with brandy, which will soften the surface of the cake.

Remove the cake from the tin, sprinkle more brandy over, and store in an airtight container for up to six months or in the refrigerator or deep-freeze for one year. Sprinkle a little brandy over the cake once a month to keep it moist.

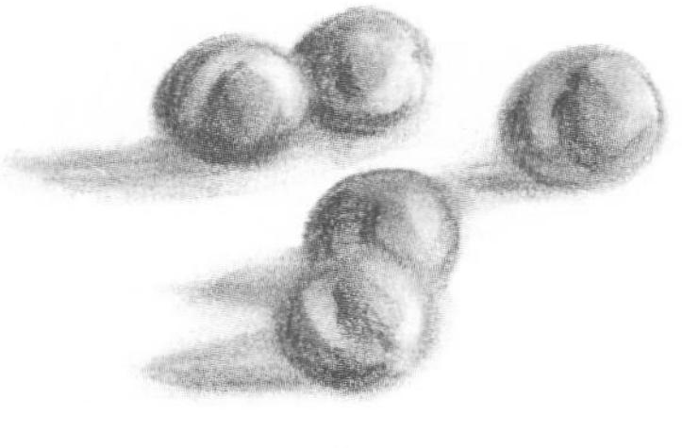

MOIST CHRISTMAS CAKE

5 x 250 ml fruit cake mix (750 g)
125 g pitted dates, finely chopped
300 ml halved glacé cherries (200 g)
125 ml chopped pecan nuts or walnuts (50 g)
125 ml brandy
250 g butter
250 ml brown sugar (200 g)
5 eggs
15 ml smooth apricot jam
500 ml Snowflake cake flour (280 g)
1 ml salt
3 ml ground nutmeg
3 ml ground cinnamon
5 ml mixed spice
5 ml ground ginger
2 ml ground cloves
3 ml bicarbonate of soda

ICING
smooth apricot jam
marzipan
ready-to-roll icing

❶ Mix cake mix, dates, cherries, nuts and brandy together and leave overnight.

❷ Cream butter and sugar together and add eggs; beat well after each addition until light and fluffy. Add jam and fruit mixture, mixing well.

❸ Add sifted dry ingredients and mix well.

❹ Line a 20 cm square cake tin with two layers brown paper or two layers greaseproof paper. Grease well, turn mixture into tin and level top of cake mixture with spatula. Bake in a preheated oven at 150 °C (300 °F) for 2¼ hours.

❺ Test centre of cake with a skewer. If baked, skewer will come out clean.

❻ Allow to cool completely in tin. Turn out and remove lining. Sprinkle with brandy; seal with plastic wrap.

❼ Store in a cool place. Sprinkle brandy over cake once a month.

❽ Spread thin layer of jam over entire cake. Cover with marzipan and ice with ready-to-roll icing or Royal Icing (page 67).

BOILED FRUIT CAKE

850 ml dried fruit cake mix (500 g)
165 ml halved glacé cherries (100 g)
250 ml sugar (200 g)
100 g butter or margarine
250 ml water
500 ml Snowflake cake flour (280 g)
10 ml bicarbonate of soda
2 ml salt
1 egg, beaten
65 ml brandy

❶ Boil cake mix, cherries, sugar, butter and water together for about 10 minutes. Leave to cool.

❷ Sift the flour, bicarbonate of soda and salt together and stir into the fruit mixture.

❸ Mix in beaten egg and brandy. Line a 20 cm round, loose-bottomed cake tin with one layer brown paper or three layers greaseproof paper. Grease well and turn mixture into tin.

❹ Bake in a preheated oven at 150 °C (300 °F) for 1¼ hours. Test centre of cake with a skewer. If baked, skewer will come out clean. Leave in turned-off oven for a while to prevent sinking. Remove from oven.

❺ Allow to cool completely in tin before turning out. Sprinkle with brandy and seal. Allow to mature for at least 2 weeks.

VARIATIONS

If you run out of brandy or do not wish to use it, substitute pure apricot juice. It preserves just as well.

For individual fruit cakes: Turn mixture into three 12 cm round ovenproof bowls and bake in a preheated oven at 150 °C (300 °F) for 45 minutes.

TIP

If the top of your fruit cake is a little too crusty for your taste, cover it with a layer of sliced raw apple. Leave in an airtight container for 24 hours. After a day the crust will become soft and moist and the apple slices can be removed.

Clockwise from top: Christmas Tree Biscuits, Boiled Fruit Cake and Moist Christmas Cake.

CHRISTMAS TREE BISCUITS

125 g margarine
125 ml castor sugar (105 g)
5 ml vanilla essence
1 egg
500 ml Snowflake cake flour (280 g)
65 ml cornflour (30 g)
5 ml baking powder
3 ml salt
Glacé Icing (page 67)

❶ Beat margarine and sugar together. Add essence and egg and beat until light and fluffy.

❷ Sift dry ingredients, add to creamed mixture and knead to form a stiff dough.

❸ Roll out to a thickness of 4 mm and, using a Christmas biscuit cutter, cut into shapes. If hanging the biscuits from a tree, make a hole in the dough.

❹ Place on a greased baking tray and bake in a preheated oven at 180 °C (350 °F) for 10–15 minutes, or until light brown on the edges.

❺ Remove biscuits from tray using a spatula; place on a wire rack to cool.

❻ Ice with Glacé Icing and decorate with silver balls, and so on. Christmas biscuits may also be dipped into melted chocolate before decorating.

Makes about 40

TIP

For hanging biscuits, make a hole for the ribbon with an icing nozzle.

STEAMED PUDDINGS

Steamed sponge puddings, traditionally eaten at Christmas time, have a finer texture than baked sponge cakes. They are usually steamed in a cloth, but are equally good steamed in a metal bowl.

Preparing the bowl

Grease the inside of the bowl and line the base with greaseproof paper. Place a topping such as fruit on the bottom and fill the bowl to about 5 cm from the top. Cover with greaseproof paper, then seal with metal lid to prevent water from entering. Then place the bowl on a wire rack in a saucepan so that it does not touch the bottom of the pot. This will ensure even cooking.

Steaming and reheating

Christmas puddings are steamed for at least 2 hours and can be kept, sealed, for 2–3 months. Reheat by steaming over a saucepan for 30 minutes or heat in a preheated oven at 180 °C (350 °F) for 30 minutes.

TRADITIONAL CHRISTMAS PUDDING

250 ml raisins (150 g)
250 ml brandy or sherry
250 g butter
250 ml sugar (200 g)
4 eggs
250 ml Snowflake cake flour (140 g)
10 ml bicarbonate of soda
2 ml salt
10 ml ground cinnamon
3 ml ground ginger
3 ml ground nutmeg
2 ml allspice
150 g pitted dates, chopped
250 ml currants (150 g)
250 ml chopped pecan nuts (100 g)
250 ml finely grated raw carrot (125 g)
250 ml fresh breadcrumbs (60 g)
50 ml golden syrup
15 ml grated lemon rind
15 ml grated orange rind

❶ Soak raisins in brandy or sherry overnight.

❷ Beat butter and sugar together. Add eggs, one at a time, beating well after each addition.

❸ Sift dry ingredients together, add to creamed mixture, and mix well. Add remaining ingredients and raisins.

❹ Spoon mixture into a greased 2-litre (8-cup) metal pudding bowl. Cover with a double layer of tin foil or greaseproof paper and secure with string or a metal top.

❺ Place on a wire rack in a large saucepan and pour in boiling water, to reach halfway up sides of bowl.

❻ Steam for 2½–3 hours, or until well cooked, remembering to check water level and refill if necessary.

❼ Allow to stand in bowl for at least 20 minutes before removing.

❽ Serve hot with brandy sauce or cream.

Serves 8–10

TIPS

To reheat, steam pudding for 30 minutes as directed in the recipe.

Place a tea towel over the top of the bowl before placing the lid on the saucepan, as this absorbs the condensation and prevents the pudding from going soggy.

To form a handle: Cover bowl with layers of greaseproof paper and tie with string just below the rim. Also form a loop above the bowl. This will serve as a useful handle.

Brandy Sauce

30 ml butter
250 ml castor sugar (210 g)
50 ml brandy
2 eggs, separated
125 ml fresh cream or milk

❶ Using a double boiler, melt butter while gradually beating in sugar.

❷ Add brandy, beat well, and add egg yolks and cream.

❸ Cook until thickened.

❹ Beat egg whites and fold in lightly until smooth. Serve hot.

MINCE PIES

These pies were originally made in an oval shape to symbolize Christ's crib.

1 quantity Cream Cheese Pastry (page 34) OR 1 quantity Rich Shortcrust Pastry (page 30)
454 g jar fruit mincemeat
1 egg white
castor sugar

❶ Roll out pastry to a thickness of 3 mm. Cut out rounds to fit base of patty pan tins or bun tins. Cut the same number of smaller circles to form the lids of pies.

❷ Place 5 ml fruit mince on the base of each pastry.

❸ Dampen pastry edge with water, cover with lid, and seal. Prick holes in the lid with a fork or make a small incision with the tip of a sharp knife. Brush with lightly beaten egg white or iced water.

❹ Bake in a preheated oven at 200 °C (400 °F) for 15 minutes, or until golden brown. Sprinkle with castor sugar while still warm.

Makes 16

TIPS

Place a small piece of unsalted butter into fruit pies to prevent juice from running out when baking.

Mince pies freeze well.

Clockwise from top right: Traditional Christmas Pudding, Christmas Mincemeat Slices and Mince Pies.

CHRISTMAS MINCEMEAT SLICES

125 g margarine
50 ml castor sugar (40 g)
25 ml oil
1 egg
5 ml vanilla essence
500 ml Snowflake cake flour (280 g)
10 ml baking powder
pinch of salt
454 g jar fruit mincemeat
1 apple, peeled and grated
25 ml brandy
icing sugar for dusting

❶ Cream margarine and sugar well.

❷ Add oil, egg and essence, and beat together.

❸ Sift dry ingredients together and knead into creamed mixture to form a dough.

❹ Press half of dough into a greased 23 cm round ovenproof dish or 23 cm square cake tin.

❺ Mix fruit mincemeat, apple and brandy together and spread thickly over dough.

❻ Coarsely grate remaining dough over mincemeat.

❼ Bake in a preheated oven at 180 °C (350 °F) for 20 minutes, or until golden brown.

❽ Dust with icing sugar before slicing.

VARIATION

SHORTBREAD TART

Substitute mincemeat and grated apple with apricot jam or lemon curd.

TIP

The pastry can be kept, wrapped, in the refrigerator for 2 days.

TRADITIONAL BAKING

MANY OF THE DISHES WE ENJOY TODAY HAVE BEEN INHERITED OVER THE CENTURIES FROM THE DUTCH, THE MALAYSIANS AND THE FRENCH HUGUENOTS – AND FAVOURITE RECIPES, OFTEN CHARACTERISTIC OF A PARTICULAR REGION – HAVE BEEN PASSED DOWN FROM ONE GENERATION TO THE NEXT.
THIS CHAPTER CONTAINS A SELECTION OF TRADITIONAL SWEET TREATS THAT ARE STILL FIRM FAVOURITES TODAY.

MILK TART

The milk tart, with its puff pastry base borrowed from the French, was introduced to South Africa by the Dutch.

BASE
50 g butter
30 ml sugar
1 egg
200 ml Snowflake self-raising flour (110 g)
1 ml salt
15 ml milk

FILLING
500 ml milk
75 ml sugar (60 g)
150 ml Snowflake cake flour (80 g)
2 eggs, separated
1 ml salt
25 ml butter
5 ml vanilla essence
ground cinnamon

❶ For base: Beat butter and sugar together. Add egg and beat until light and fluffy. Sift flour and salt together; add, with milk, to the creamed mixture.

❷ Grease a 23 cm ovenproof tart dish and press the dough into it using a spatula.

❸ For filling: Heat milk and sugar together in a heavy-based saucepan.

❹ Add some of the warm milk to flour and return to saucepan. Add egg yolks and salt.

❺ Boil until thickened, stirring frequently. Remove from heat, add butter and vanilla essence, and fold in lightly beaten egg whites.

❻ Pour into base, sprinkle with cinnamon, and bake in a preheated oven at 180 °C (350 °F) for 30 minutes.

TIP

Do not overbeat egg whites.

HERTZOG-KOEKIES

500 ml Snowflake cake flour (280 g)
10 ml baking powder
1 ml salt
50 ml castor sugar (40 g)
125 g margarine
3 large eggs, separated
50 ml water
200 g smooth apricot jam
300 ml sugar (240 g)
500 ml desiccated coconut (160 g)

❶ Sift the flour, baking powder and salt together. Add castor sugar and rub in margarine.

❷ Beat egg yolks and water together and add to dry ingredients, mixing to form a soft dough.

❸ Roll dough out thinly and press out circles. Line the base of greased patty pan tins with dough circles.

❹ Spoon a teaspoonful of apricot jam onto middle of each circle of dough.

❺ Beat egg whites until soft peak stage. Add the 300 ml sugar gradually, while still beating. Add coconut and spoon egg mixture onto apricot jam filling.

❻ Bake in a preheated oven at 180 °C (350 °F) for 20–25 minutes. Turn onto a wire rack to cool.

Makes 25–30

TIP

When making jam tarts, put spoonfuls of apricot jam into a plastic bag containing flour. Shake the bag until the jam is well coated with flour, then place onto pastry. This will ensure that the jam does not 'leak' during baking.

SOUSKLUITJIES (CINNAMON DUMPLINGS)

250 ml Snowflake cake flour (140 g)
10 ml baking powder
2 ml salt
50 ml margarine or butter
1 egg
100 ml milk
500 ml boiling water
25 ml margarine or butter
cinnamon sugar

❶ Sift the dry ingredients together. Rub in 50 ml margarine until mixture resembles breadcrumbs.

❷ Beat egg and milk together, stir into flour, and mix to a soft dough. Add extra milk if necessary.

❸ Bring water and 25 ml margarine to boil. Place spoonfuls of dough in boiling water. Cover with lid and allow to boil for 15 minutes. Do not remove lid while cooking.

❹ Remove dumplings with a slotted spoon and place in a serving dish. Sprinkle with cinnamon sugar.

❺ Bring water in which dumplings were cooked to the boil again. Add more cinnamon sugar and pour over dumplings. More water can be added if necessary.

Serves 4

TIP

Before rubbing into flour, chill butter or margarine until very hard, and grate coarsely. This will save time and result in a light texture.

Clockwise from top: Hertzogkoekies, Souskluitjies (Cinnamon Dumplings) and Milk Tart.

SOETKOEKIES

Originally, soetkoekies were decorated with 'rooi bolus' – a red powder mixed with the dough.

750 ml Snowflake cake flour (420 g)
5 ml salt
5 ml ground cloves
5 ml ground mixed spice
5 ml ground cinnamon
5 ml bicarbonate of soda
250 ml sugar (200 g)
125 g butter
125 g lard
2 eggs, beaten
125 ml sweet red wine

❶ Sift dry ingredients together and add sugar.

❷ Rub in butter and lard until mixture resembles breadcrumbs.

❸ Add beaten eggs and red wine and mix to a soft dough.

❹ Leave to stand a few hours, or overnight if possible.

❺ Roll out to a thickness of 3 mm and cut out cookies with a cookie cutter.

❻ Place on a greased baking tray and bake in a preheated oven at 200 °C (400 °F) for 10–12 minutes.

Makes about 80, depending on size

MOSBOLLETJIES

Mosbolletjies are buns originating from the Cape winelands, where they were made from dough leavened with must or mos – the juice of the grape in the first stages of fermentation – instead of yeast. If fresh grapes were not available, raisins were used instead.

500 ml raisins with seeds (300 g)
about 600 ml lukewarm water
2,5 kg Snowflake cake flour
800 ml warm milk
375 g butter
15 ml salt
400 ml sugar (320 g)
30 ml whole aniseed

❶ Chop raisins in a food processor. Add lukewarm water and leave, covered, to ferment for four days. When raisins have risen to the surface, the yeast – or must – is ready.

❷ Strain yeast through a muslin cloth and reserve liquid to make yeast mixture rise. Discard raisins.

❸ Prepare yeast sponge mixture by adding 250 ml of the flour to liquid and mixing to a thin batter. Beat slightly, cover, and leave in a warm place until double in size.

❹ Add warm milk to butter and allow to stand.

❺ Sift the remaining flour and salt together. Add sugar, butter mixture, yeast mixture and aniseed, mixing well. Add more milk if necessary.

❻ Brush surface of dough with melted butter, cover, and leave to rise in a warm place overnight.

❼ Knock down, cover, and again leave to rise in a warm place until dough has doubled in size.

❽ Shape dough into balls and pack tightly in greased deep loaf tins. Brush with melted butter. Leave in a warm place to rise until double in size.

❾ Bake in a preheated oven at 180 °C (350 °F) for about 1 hour, until golden brown.

Makes about 160 mosbolletjies depending on size

TIP

A mixer with a dough hook is ideal for making mosbolletjies.

MELKKOS

A traditional dish with a lumpy texture that is cooked with milk and flour and served with cinnamon sugar as a light meal.

2 litres milk
300 ml Snowflake cake flour (165 g)
5 ml salt
15 ml margarine or butter
cinnamon sugar

❶ Bring milk to the boil.

❷ Sift the flour and salt together and rub in margarine. Add to milk and beat. Lumps will form, but keep stirring well.

❸ Cover with lid and simmer for 5–8 minutes, until cooked.

❹ Serve hot with cinnamon sugar.

Serves 4

VETKOEK

500 ml Snowflake self-raising flour (280 g)
2 ml salt
25 ml sugar
1 egg, beaten
about 275 ml milk or water
cooking oil for deep-frying

❶ Sift flour and salt together and add sugar.

❷ Mix egg and water together and stir into dry ingredients. Mix until a sticky dough is formed.

❸ Deep-fry spoonfuls of dough in hot oil until golden brown on both sides. Drain on paper towels.

❹ Serve with butter and syrup or honey.

Makes 20

TIP

Vetkoek should preferably be eaten on the same day as cooked.

Clockwise from top: Mosbolletjies, Melkkos, Soetkoekies and Vetkoek .

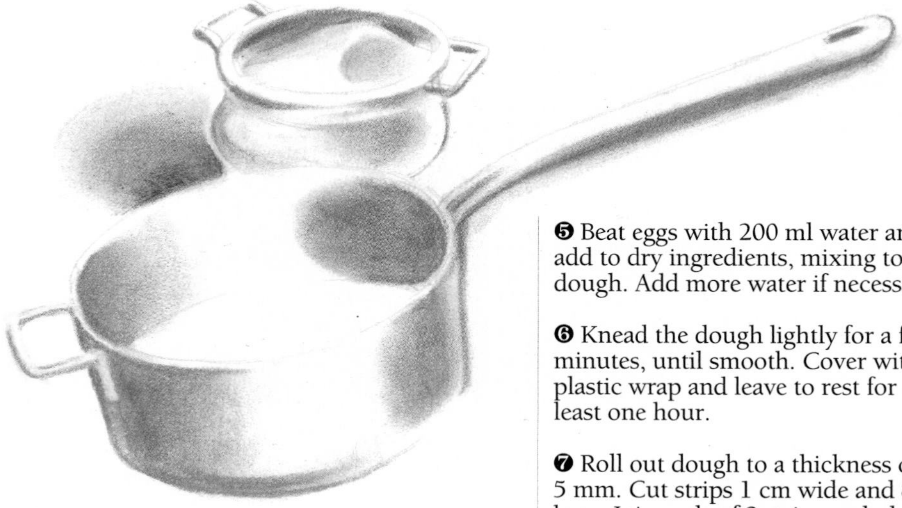

KOEKSISTERS

SYRUP
6 x 250 ml sugar (1,2 kg)
750 ml water
3 ml cream of tartar
5 ml cold water
3 ml ground ginger
1 cinnamon stick OR
1 ml ground cinnamon
rind of one lemon
20 ml lemon juice

DOUGH
4 x 250 ml Snowflake cake flour (560 g)
20 ml baking powder
5 ml salt
30 ml margarine
15 ml sugar
2 eggs
about 200 ml water
cooking oil for frying

❶ For syrup: In a large saucepan, dissolve the sugar in the water and bring to the boil.

❷ Mix cream of tartar and cold water together and add to the syrup. Add ginger, cinnamon, lemon rind and lemon juice.

❸ Boil for 10 minutes and leave to cool. Refrigerate until very cold – overnight, if possible.

❹ For dough: Sift dry ingredients together. Rub in margarine until the mixture resembles fine breadcrumbs. Add sugar.

❺ Beat eggs with 200 ml water and add to dry ingredients, mixing to a soft dough. Add more water if necessary.

❻ Knead the dough lightly for a few minutes, until smooth. Cover with plastic wrap and leave to rest for at least one hour.

❼ Roll out dough to a thickness of 5 mm. Cut strips 1 cm wide and 8 cm long. Join ends of 3 strips and plait. Alternatively, take two strips 15 cm long, join ends and roll.

❽ Deep-fry koeksisters in oil until brown on both sides. Dip immediately into ice cold syrup, making sure that the koeksister is soaked through.

❾ Remove with a slotted spoon and turn onto a wire rack. If syrup becomes warm, return to the refrigerator. Store koeksisters in the refrigerator before serving.

Makes 48

TIPS

Do not fry koeksisters too quickly or the outside will be cooked, and the inside still raw.

Use two bowls of syrup. Keep one in the refrigerator while using the other.

Keep koeksisters in the deep-freeze and remove 30 minutes before use.

BROWN PUDDING

1 egg
125 ml sugar (100 g)
15 ml smooth apricot jam
250 ml Snowflake cake flour (140 g)
5 ml baking powder
5 ml bicarbonate of soda
1 ml salt
20 ml vinegar
250 ml milk

SYRUP
250 ml sugar (200 g)
250 ml milk
125 ml boiling water
50 g butter
5 ml vanilla essence

❶ Beat egg and sugar together until light and fluffy.

❷ Add remaining ingredients, except milk, beating well. Beat in milk and pour mixture into a greased, medium-sized ovenproof dish. Bake in a preheated oven at 180 °C (350 °F) for 40–50 minutes.

❸ For syrup: Boil all ingredients except essence in a saucepan for 5 minutes. Add essence.

❹ Spoon syrup over hot pudding.

Serves 4–6

TIPSY TART

60 g margarine
200 ml sugar (160 g)
250 g pitted dates, chopped
375 ml boiling water
5 ml bicarbonate of soda
2 eggs
375 ml Snowflake cake flour (210 g)
5 ml baking powder
2 ml salt
125 ml chopped walnuts (50 g)

SYRUP
250 ml sugar (200 g)
125 ml water
60 g margarine
5 ml vanilla essence
75 ml brandy

❶ Mix margarine, sugar, dates and boiling water with bicarbonate of soda in a mixing bowl and leave to cool. Beat eggs and add to mixture.

❷ Sift flour, baking powder and salt together and add, with nuts, to date mixture. Mix well.

❸ Spoon into a greased ovenproof dish and bake in a preheated oven at 180 °C (350 °F) for 30 minutes.

❹ For syrup: Boil sugar, water and margarine together for 15 minutes. Add essence and brandy.

❺ Remove tart from oven; pour syrup over. Serve with cream or custard.

Clockwise from top right: Tipsy Tart, Pumpkin Fritters and Koeksisters.

PUMPKIN FRITTERS

500 ml cooked, mashed pumpkin (about 450 g)
125 ml Snowflake cake flour (70 g)
5 ml baking powder
2 ml salt
2 eggs, beaten
about 30 ml milk
cinnamon sugar
cooking oil for frying

❶ Mix pumpkin, flour, baking powder and salt together.

❷ Add eggs and enough milk to form a batter.

❸ Shallow-fry spoonfuls of mixture in hot oil on both sides, until brown.

❹ Drain on paper towels and sprinkle with cinnamon sugar.

Makes 18, depending on size

TIP

To make cinnamon sugar, mix 100 ml sugar with 10 ml ground cinnamon.

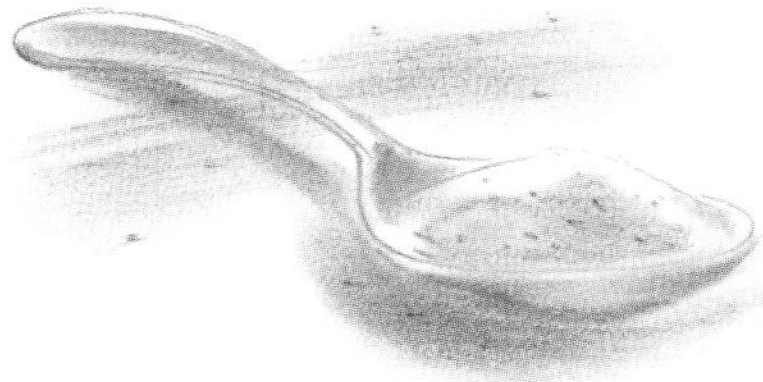

12

BAKING FOR CHILDREN

MOST CHILDREN REACH A STAGE WHEN THEY WANT TO GET INVOLVED IN BAKING. THE RECIPES INCLUDED IN THE FIRST SECTION OF THIS CHAPTER ARE IDEAL FOR CHILDREN TO MAKE BY THEMSELVES, WITH A LITTLE SUPERVISION IF NECESSARY, OR EVEN FOR YOU TO QUICKLY PUT TOGETHER.
BIRTHDAY CAKES, COVERED IN THE SECOND SECTION, ARE ALWAYS THE HIGHLIGHT OF THE PARTY AND NEEDN'T BE TIME-CONSUMING OR DIFFICULT TO MAKE. WITH A LITTLE IMAGINATION, A BASIC SPONGE CAN BE TURNED INTO SOMETHING SPECIAL – AND THE BIRTHDAY GIRL OR BOY WILL ENJOY HELPING WITH THE DECORATING.

For the small baker

CUP CAKES

125 g margarine
200 ml castor sugar (170 g)
5 ml vanilla essence
2 eggs
500 ml Snowflake self-raising flour (280 g)
2 ml salt
200 ml milk
whipped cream
castor sugar
icing sugar

❶ Place 24 paper cookie cases on a baking sheet or in muffin tins.

❷ Cream margarine and sugar until smooth and creamy. Add essence and eggs, beating well after each addition. Fold in sifted flour and salt alternately with milk.

❸ Spoon into paper cases until three-quarters full. Bake in a preheated oven at 200 °C (400 °F) for 12–15 minutes.

❹ To make butterfly cakes, cut a thin slice from the top of each cup cake, and cut slice in half down centre. Beat cream stiffly with a little castor sugar. Place cream on top of each cake.

❺ Place cut tops on cream to resemble wings, and dust with icing sugar.

Makes 24

VARIATION

ORANGE CUP CAKES

Add 5 ml orange essence and 10 ml grated orange rind to mixture.

TIP

Ice cakes with Glacé Icing (page 67).

GINGERBREAD MEN

125 g butter
125 ml brown sugar (100 g)
1 egg yolk
500 ml Snowflake cake flour (280 g)
5 ml bicarbonate of soda
10 ml ground ginger
5 ml ground cinnamon
50 ml golden syrup
40–50 ml water

ROYAL ICING
1 egg white
375 ml icing sugar (200 g)
food colouring

❶ Cream butter and sugar until light and fluffy. Add egg yolk and beat well.

❷ Sift dry ingredients together and add, with syrup and enough water, to make a stiff dough. Roll dough to a thickness of about 4 mm and cut gingerbread figures with a special cutter.

❸ Place on greased trays and bake in a preheated oven at 180 °C (350 °F) for 10 minutes. Turn onto a wire rack to cool.

❹ For icing: Lightly beat egg white. Gradually add sifted icing sugar, beating well. Beat to piping consistency and add food colouring of choice. Pipe detail on gingerbread figures.

Makes 12, depending on size of cutter

VARIATION

Royal icing can be substituted with raisins or chocolate chips for the eyes and buttons. Cut strips of cherry for the mouth.

TIP

Cutters with different shapes and sizes are available from kitchen shops. If unable to get a suitable one, draw your own shape of a man or a woman on a piece of stiff cardboard and cut out. Place shape on rolled out dough and cut around it with a sharp knife.

CHOCOLATE CHIP CRUNCHIES

250 g butter or margarine
250 ml sugar (200 g)
250 ml Snowflake brown bread meal (140 g)
2 ml salt
500 ml rolled oats (160 g)
250 ml coconut (80 g)
200 ml chocolate chips (140 g)
30 ml golden syrup
5 ml vanilla essence
2 ml bicarbonate of soda
50 ml boiling water

❶ Cream butter and sugar together.

❷ Sift brown bread meal and salt and add bran left behind in sieve.

❸ Add to creamed mixture with oats, coconut, chocolate chips, syrup and essence.

❹ Dissolve bicarbonate of soda in water and add, mixing well.

❺ Place teaspoonfuls of mixture on a greased baking tray and flatten with a spoon. Leave enough space for spreading during baking.

❻ Bake in a preheated oven at 180 °C (350 °F) for 15 minutes.

Makes about 60

VARIATIONS

Substitute chocolate with raisins.

Substitute oats with rice crispies.

Clockwise from top left: Chocolate Chip Crunchies, Jam Slices, Cup Cakes, Butterfly Cakes and Gingerbread Men.

JAM SLICES

125 g margarine
125 ml sugar (100 g)
1 egg
5 ml vanilla essence
500 ml Snowflake cake flour (280 g)
10 ml baking powder
about 125 ml smooth apricot jam (about 160 g)
icing sugar

❶ Beat margarine and sugar well.

❷ Add egg and essence and beat until light and fluffy. Add sifted dry ingredients and knead well.

❸ Press half the dough into a greased 20 cm x 24 cm rectangular tin. Spread a layer of jam over dough.

❹ Coarsely grate remaining dough over jam.

❺ Bake in a preheated oven at 180 °C (350 °F) for 20 minutes, or until golden brown. Leave for a few minutes to cool. Cut into squares and leave to cool in pan. Dust with icing sugar.

Makes 20, depending on size

PLAY DOUGH

500 ml Snowflake cake flour (280 g)
500 ml water
125 ml table salt (140 g)
15 ml cream of tartar
15 ml cooking oil
4–5 ml food colouring of choice

❶ Mix together all ingredients except food colouring in a heavy-based saucepan. Stir over medium heat until mixture forms a ball in the middle.

❷ Leave to cool and knead well. Add colouring and knead again.

❸ Keep in an airtight container or plastic bag to prevent drying out.

TIPS

Dip a skewer into food colouring and shake drops from skewer onto dough to achieve desired colour.

Return dough to the plastic bag or airtight container to ensure that it lasts longer and does not dry out.

Birthday cakes

Serve birthday cakes on a cake board covered with paper or foil, and decorated with desiccated coconut, sweets, popcorn, hundreds-and-thousands, flakes, or even confetti.

TREASURE CHEST

2 x Chocolate Oil Cake (page 50)
Chocolate Butter Icing (page 66)
chocolate coins
costume jewellery
sweets

❶ Follow basic recipe for chocolate cake, using two 23 cm loaf tins. For layer 1, fill one-third full and bake 20 minutes. For layer 2, fill two-thirds full and bake 40–45 minutes.

❷ Assemble using icing as shown in illustration. Ice cake and decorate as shown in photograph.

HANSEL AND GRETEL

2 x Hot Milk Sponge Cake (page 57)
smooth apricot jam
Basic Icing (page 66)
food colouring of choice
liquorice strips
Smarties
wafer biscuits
chocolate flakes
desiccated coconut

❶ Follow basic recipe for sponge cake, but bake in two 23 cm loaf tins for 50–55 minutes.

❷ Cut cooled cake and assemble using apricot jam, as shown in illustration. Ice cake and decorate as shown in photograph.

> *Tip*
>
> *To colour desiccated coconut: Sprinkle on a tray and mix in a few drops of desired colouring. Leave to dry.*

Trim layer 1 to form the lid and attach to layer 2 with icing

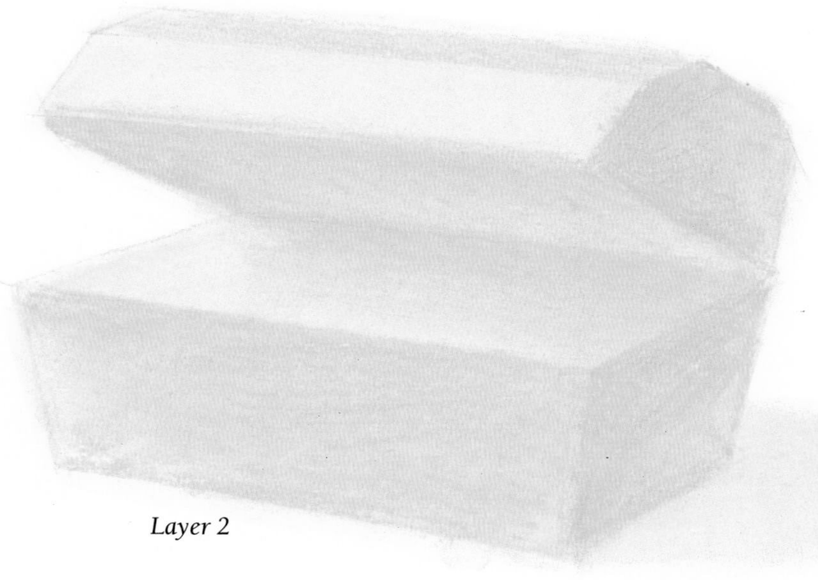

Trim one of the loaves to form the roof, then attach the roof to the house using apricot jam

Treasure Chest Cake.

Hansel and Gretel Cake.

MICKEY MOUSE CAKE

2 x 20 cm Hot Milk Sponge Cake layers (page 57)
½ quantity Basic Icing (page 66)
½ quantity Chocolate Butter Icing (page 66)
chocolate rounds
chocolate vermicelli
liquorice strips
fruit drop for mouth

❶ Follow basic recipe for sponge cake.

❷ Cut cooled cake and assemble using icing, as shown in illustrations.

❸ Ice cake and decorate as shown in photograph.

> *TIP*
>
> *For a darker icing, substitute butter in icing with white margarine.*

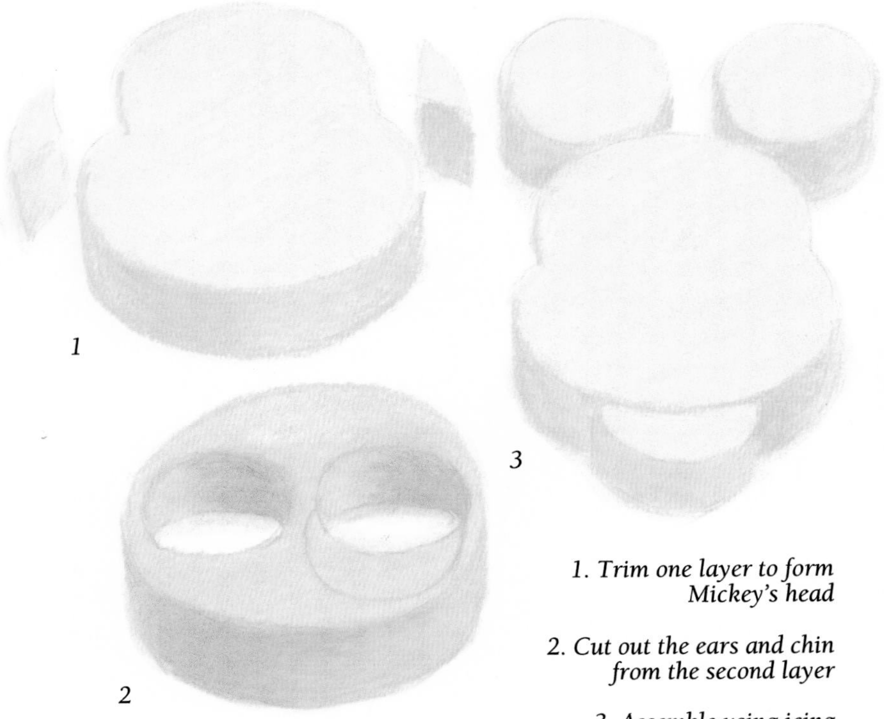

1. Trim one layer to form Mickey's head

2. Cut out the ears and chin from the second layer

3. Assemble using icing

DINOSAUR

2 x 20 cm Chocolate Oil Cake layers (page 50)
smooth apricot jam
Chocolate Butter Icing (page 66)
wafer biscuits
flat round chocolates
Smarties
Choc Stix
liquorice strips
hundreds-and-thousands
desiccated coconut

❶ Cut cooled cake and assemble using apricot jam or icing, as shown in illustrations.

❷ Ice cake and decorate as shown in photograph.

> *TIP*
>
> *To make round flat chocolates: Melt dark cooking chocolate over saucepan of boiling water, stirring occasionally. Spread smoothly onto greaseproof paper. Allow to set and cut out rounds.*

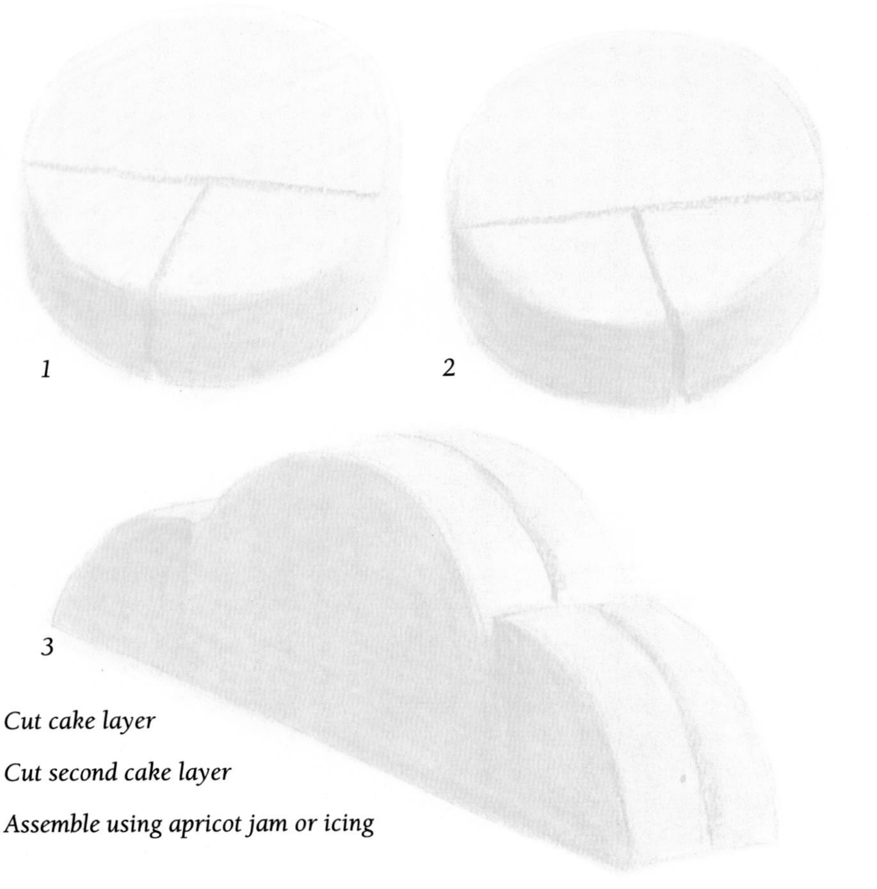

1. Cut cake layer

2. Cut second cake layer

3. Assemble using apricot jam or icing

Mickey Mouse Cake.

Dinosaur Cake.

DEALING WITH FLOPS

Unfortunately, flops are a reality that even the best cook has to face! However, a flop needn't be the end of the world, and, with a little patience and imagination, can probably be salvaged.

Here we give you a few ideas as to what to do with cakes that don't meet your expectations. Some are suitable for cakes that have fallen apart; others for cakes that haven't risen.

Make petits fours

Cut the cake into 3 cm x 3 cm squares and sandwich pairs of squares together with apricot jam. Follow instructions given for Petits Fours (page 58).

Make a gâteau

Cut the cake horizontally into four layers. Pour 15 ml sherry onto layers. Spread two of the layers with confectioner's custard (page 43) and the remaining two layers with whipped cream. Assemble the cake, starting with a custard layer and ending with a cream layer. Decorate the cake with cream, grated chocolate and other appropriate decorations.

Make a ring cake

If the cake has sunk in the centre, cut out the centre and make a ring cake. Fill with fresh fruit, then ice and decorate.

Make lamingtons

Cut the cake into large squares. Follow the recipe given for Lamingtons (page 60).

Make a trifle

Use large squares of sponge cake and follow the recipe given for trifle (page 102).

Use smaller offcuts from cakes for making crumbs and use them as you would breadcrumbs, or bake them in the oven until golden brown and serve with cream or custard. Smaller crumbs can be used for making truffles or in steam puddings.

Cake flaws

FLAW	REASON FOR FLAW
Cake rises to a point	Over-manipulation Batter too stiff Initial oven temperature too high
Surface of cake not level	Uneven heat penetration (pans touch each other or oven sides) Oven not level
Cake sinks in middle	Too much sugar used Batter too dry Under-manipulation Pan too small Oven temperature too low Cake moved during baking Cake not cooked Oven door opened during baking Too much raising agent used
Cake does not rise	Tins too large Inactive raising agent Ingredients too cold
Mixture runs over the top	Tins too small Too much raising agent used Too much sugar used
Cake rises and sinks while in oven	Too much liquid used Too much raising agent used Oven door opened too soon/too frequently
Cake sticks to baking tin	Left in tin too long Too much sugar used Tin not greased
Cake breaks when removed from tin	Cake removed from oven before set Too much raising agent used Cake removed from tin carelessly
Speckled top crust	Air bubbles break on surface as a result of too much air having been incorporated into mixture Sugar not dissolved or too coarse
Cracked top crust	Mixture too stiff Initial oven temperature too high
Moist, sticky crust	Too much sugar used Mixture too runny Underbaked
Crisp upper crust	Too much sugar used Too much shortening used Too much raising agent used
Coarse, grainy texture	Too much raising agent used Insufficient creaming of ingredients
Dry and crumbly texture	Baked too long at low temperature Too much raising agent used
Heavy, compact texture	Ingredients too cold Mixture too soft Insufficient/flat raising agent Flour not folded in
Tunnels and large holes	Ingredients overmixed Oven temperature too high
Sunken fruit mixture	Fruit wet or damp – toss in flour to coat Mixture too soft to support weight of fruit Too much raising agent used

A

Al dente The Italian term describing the texture of pasta when it is cooked: tender but firm to the bite.

B

Bain-marie An oven pan half-filled with hot water in which soufflés, terrines, and so on are baked at 90–95 °C (about 180 °F).
Bake blind Baking flan or tartlet cases without filling, to colour and crisp the pastry.
Baking powder A raising agent consisting of an alkali and an acid. Largely, it comprises cream of tartar and bicarbonate of soda, in the proportion of 1 teaspoon cream of tartar to ½ teaspoon bicarbonate of soda. This is equal to 2 teaspoons of baking powder.
Beat Mixing ingredients to introduce air, making the mixture lighter and fluffier, using a wooden spoon, hand whisk or electric mixer.
Béchamel A basic white sauce.
Biscuit cutter A metal cutter, usually round, used for cutting shapes out of dough for making biscuits.
Blanch Loosening skins of nuts and vegetables by plunging them first into hot water and then into cold water.
Blend Obtaining equal distribution of ingredients by gently mixing with a spoon, beater or liquidizer.
Bouchée A small patty of puff pastry, without a lid, containing a savoury or sweet filling.
Bouquet garni A small bunch of herbs (usually parsley, thyme and a bayleaf) tied together, or in a small muslin bag, and used to flavour stews, soups and casseroles.
Bran The outer layer or husk of the cereal grain; a major source of fibre.

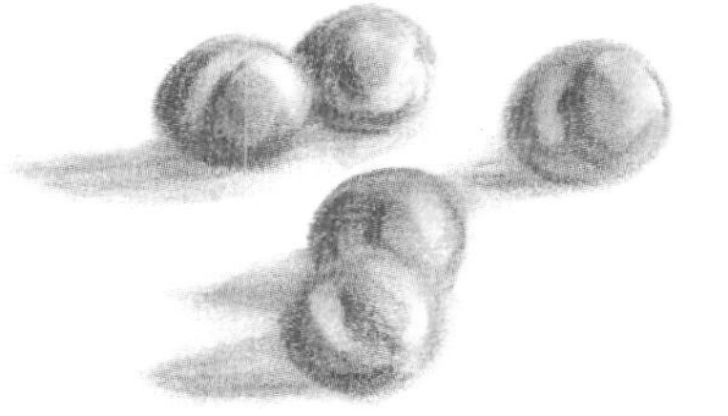

C

Cannelloni Large tubes of pasta, stuffed with savoury fillings.
Caramelize To cook sugar syrup or sugar until brown and syrupy.
Choc bits (Morsels) Small buds of dark chocolate, available in 250 g packets, that do not melt when cooked in biscuits and cakes.
Creaming The process of mixing shortening and another solid such as sugar or flour.
Cream of tartar One of the acid components of baking powder, in which two parts are mixed with one part bicarbonate of soda.
Cream puff A hollowed-out puff made from soft choux pastry, baked at high temperature, and filled with whipped cream or custard.
Crêpes Thin, light pancakes.
Crêpes suzette Thin crêpes cooked in orange sauce and flamed in brandy or liqueur.
Croissants Crescent-shaped rolls.
Cup cakes Small cakes baked in paper cases.

D

Dissolve To make or become liquid, especially by immersion or dispersion in a liquid.
Dumplings Small balls of dough made from flour, semolina, cornflour, potato, soft cheese or even stiffly beaten egg whites. Dumplings can be steamed on top of a stew or casserole, simmered in stock or baked. Sweet dumplings are simmered in syrup.

E

Éclair A long, hollow finger-shaped puff made from soft choux pastry, filled with cream and usually topped with melted chocolate.
Egg wash Beaten egg, usually diluted with water, used to produce a glazed surface on baked goods.
Essence Compounds used for flavouring sweets, confectionery, and so on. They can be either natural, synthetic or blends of both.

F

Fettuccine Also called tagliatelle. A fairly broad ribbon noodle pasta that may be white or green (with spinach added). Usually purchased coiled into 'nest' shapes.
Flake To separate cooked food, especially fish, with two forks.
Flan An open, round pastry case filled with fruit that is later glazed.
Flambé To cook food by tossing in a pan to which burning brandy or other alcohol is added.
Flapjack A griddle cake or crumpet.
Florentines Thin biscuits made of nuts, glacé fruit and chocolate.
Fold in To gently incorporate an ingredient into a mixture. When making a sponge cake, folding in the flour with a large metal spoon or spatula is the gentlest way to incorporate it into the batter.
Fruit cake A cake containing a large amount of dried fruits and nuts and only enough batter to bind them together. Usually no raising agent is added.
Fry Cooking in hot fat. Deep-frying involves cooking food such as doughnuts in at least 80 mm hot fat; food such as fish cakes is shallow-fried in a little oil in a shallow pan.

G

Garnish To add decorative or tasty touches to food.
Gâteau The French word for any kind of cake. In other parts of the world the word 'gâteau' is synonymous with a rich, lightly

decorated cake, often layered and including liqueur, and decorated with cream, chocolate, nuts or fruit.
GÉNOISE Good-quality plain cake or sponge that consists of eggs, sugar, flour and melted butter that is used for filled cakes, petits fours and baked Alaska. It is baked in a flat tin.
GLAZE To impart a gloss by brushing pastry with egg and milk to give the surface a shiny, attractive appearance.
GLUTEN The protein in flour that is developed when dough is kneaded, making it elastic.

I

ICING Sugar mixtures used for coating and decorative purposes.

K

KNEAD To work dough into a mass by folding over, pressing and squeezing.

M

MARZIPAN A confection, made from almond paste, sugar and egg whites, used for modelling fruits, figures, and so on.
MERINGUE Egg whites and sugar whipped to a stiff, frothy white mass.
MOCHA A flavour made from coffee and chocolate or cocoa.
MOULD Shaping of a dough or mixture.
MOZZARELLA CHEESE A soft, unripened white Italian cheese that goes particularly well with tomatoes. This is a low-fat cheese with a compact, elastic texture that is often used as the cheese base for pizzas.

P

PASTA Paste made with flour and water and sometimes enriched with egg and oil. Used to make macaroni, spaghetti, and so on.
PASTY Small pastry pie containing meat and vegetables.
PASTRY WHEEL A metal wheel that is used for cutting pastry into various shapes.
PETITS FOURS A variety of tiny sponge cakes, iced and decorated, which are served with coffee after dessert.
PHYLLO PASTRY A paper-thin pastry made from flour and water that can conveniently be bought from supermarkets or bakeries. Each layer is brushed with melted butter before baking. Remaining sheets of phyllo should be covered with a damp tea towel to prevent them drying out.
PIPING BAG A bag fitted with a small metal nozzle, through which cream, icing and other pastes are forced for the purpose of decorating dishes.
POPPY SEEDS The tiny whole grey seeds of the poppy plant used for sprinkling on bread, rolls and savoury biscuits before baking. Also used as an ingredient in cakes.
PROVE Allowing dough to rise before baking.

R

ROUX Flour and fat cooked into a thick mixture and used as a base for many sauces.
RUB IN To combine shortening and dry ingredients by rubbing them lightly with the fingertips until the mixture resembles fine breadcrumbs.

S

SAUTÉ To fry food rapidly in a small amount of fat until it is evenly browned, shaking the pan to toss and turn the contents. The food is either just browned or cooked through.
SAVARIN A rich yeast cake which is baked in a ring mould and soaked in liqueur-flavoured syrup. Served cold with cream.
SEASON To add salt, pepper, spices or herbs to enhance the flavour of food.
SELF-RAISING FLOUR White flour to which sodium bicarbonate and one or more leavening acids have been added.
SESAME SEEDS The seeds of the *sesamum indicum* plant, which have a sweet, nutty flavour; used to top breads and crackers.
SCALD To heat milk to just below boiling point.
SIFT To shake dry ingredients through a sieve to remove lumps, to aerate, and to mix.
SOUFFLÉ A light, fluffy dish consisting of a sauce thickened with egg yolks into which stiffly beaten egg whites are folded.
STRUDEL Thin leaves of filled pastry that are rolled up and baked.

T

TUILES Wafer-thin curled biscuits served with coffee or ice-cream.

V

VOL-AU-VENT Light flaky case of puff pastry with a lid, filled with a sweet or savoury filling.

W

WASH To brush goods with egg, milk or water prior to baking or to apply icing or a glaze to baked goods.
WHIP Rapid aerating by beating with a whisk.
WHISK Looped wire utensil used to beat air into batters, eggs or cream.

Y

YEAST A commercial preparation containing yeast cells, used in raising dough for bread.

Z

ZEST The outer layer of citrus fruits, which contains aromatic citrus oil, and which is used as a flavouring. It is usually thinly pared with a vegetable peeler, or grated either with a zester or on a grater to separate it from the bitter white pith beneath.

General index

This index includes information given in tips and introductions to sections and recipes; see also the Glossary, page 125. Page references in *italic* refer to photographs; those in **bold** refer to a main mention; *bis* indicates two references on a page; *ter* indicates three.

Index of recipes

Page references in *italic* refer to photographs; Var. indicates a variation of the recipe.